Singletons

IN A PLC AT WORK®

 Navigating On-Ramps to Meaningful Collaboration

BRIG LEANE & JON YOST

Solution Tree | Press

a division of
Solution Tree

555 North Morton Street
Bloomington, IN 47404
800.733.6786 (toll free) / 812.336.7700
FAX: 812.336.7790
email: info@SolutionTree.com
SolutionTree.com

Visit **go.SolutionTree.com/PLCbooks** to download the free reproducibles in this book.

Printed in the United States of America

Library of Congress Control Number: 2022019252

Solution Tree
Jeffrey C. Jones, CEO
Edmund M. Ackerman, President

Solution Tree Press
President and Publisher: Douglas M. Rife
Associate Publisher: Sarah Payne-Mills
Managing Production Editor: Kendra Slayton
Editorial Director: Todd Brakke
Art Director: Rian Anderson
Copy Chief: Jessi Finn
Senior Production Editor: Suzanne Kraszewski
Content Development Specialist: Amy Rubenstein
Copy Editor: Evie Madsen
Proofreader: Elisabeth Abrams
Cover and Text Designer: Kelsey Hoover
Associate Editor: Sarah Ludwig
Editorial Assistants: Charlotte Jones and Elijah Oates

Acknowledgments

Sincere thanks to Kim and our girls, Emily, Chloe, and Kayla; my extended Leane and Sheldahl families; my friends; and the Solution Tree family. Your encouragement continues to make a huge difference in my life. Finally, I would like to thank Jesus.

—Brig Leane

This book is dedicated to my beautiful and loving wife, Michelle, and my sons, Jordan and Tyler. Thank you, Michelle, for supporting me in every one of my ventures in public education. Thanks for understanding the time it takes and giving me that flexibility. Most of all, thank you for always believing in me and reminding me I could do anything I put my mind to. Your support has never wavered. Jordan and Tyler, thank you for being such godly, wonderful young men. The way you live your lives continuously inspires me to do my best and make a difference in this world. I can't sufficiently describe my love and appreciation for you.

I would also like to thank two leaders who guided and mentored me more than I ever deserved. Thank you, Rich Smith, for the countless mentoring sessions and always having my best interests in mind. From year one as a second-grade teacher with you as my principal to today, when you always make it a priority to "talk shop," I greatly appreciate your guidance. I'm not sure what I would do without your friendship. Thank you to Marc Johnson for giving me the opportunity to lead in Sanger Unified School District and for introducing me to Rick and Becky DuFour. Thank you for your continuous encouragement. Those years in Sanger Unified changed my life.

Finally, I want to acknowledge the Solution Tree family. I have been inspired by so many of you, and I have been blessed with so many opportunities to learn and serve alongside you. To this day, I feel like I'm living a fantasy by being allowed to be a part of the family.

—Jon Yost

Solution Tree Press would like to thank the following reviewers:

Visit **go.SolutionTree.com/PLCbooks** to
download the free reproducibles in this book.

Table of Contents

CHAPTER 4

Course-Alike On-Ramp: The Virtual Team

CHAPTER 5

Common-Content On-Ramp

CHAPTER 6

Critical-Friend On-Ramp

CHAPTER 7

Putting It All Together

About the Authors

Brig Leane, former principal of Fruita Middle School in Colorado, has been working in education since 2000. He has been an assistant principal and has taught at the middle and high school levels in inner-city, suburban, and rural schools. He has also been an adjunct professor at Colorado Christian University.

Under Brig's leadership as principal, Fruita's organizational health index grew from the lowest to the highest levels. This collaborative transformation propelled a school previously known for teacher independence to national Model Professional Learning Community (PLC) status, one of only three schools in the state to receive this designation. During the transformation, Fruita was the only middle school in the Mesa County Valley School District recognized for achieving student growth above the state median in every tested subject, in all grades, and with every demographic subgroup of students the state of Colorado measures. His school was recognized on Getting Smart's annual list as one of eighty-five schools in the United States educators should visit.

As a teacher, Brig learned the power of the PLC process firsthand, as his mathematics team academically grew students more than any other team, in any grade, in any tested subject in a 22,000-student school district.

Brig has presented to large and small groups of educators, and his work has been published in *Phi Delta Kappan*, *Principal Leadership*, and the Association for Supervision and Curriculum Development's online learning platform.

Education is Brig's second career, following his successful service as an officer in the U.S. Coast Guard, having attained the rank of lieutenant commander. He graduated with honors from the U.S. Coast Guard Academy with a bachelor's degree in civil engineering and served as an officer for many years on humanitarian missions around the United States. He was selected as a Troops-to-Teachers recipient and earned master's degrees in business administration and educational leadership from Colorado Mesa University.

To learn more about Brig's work, visit www.brigleane.com and follow @BrigLeane on Twitter.

Jon Yost has retired as associate superintendent of curriculum and instruction for Sanger Unified School District in California. He has worked in public education at the elementary, secondary, and district levels since 1990. He has also been an adjunct professor at California State University, Fresno.

Jon has led and fostered the deep implementation of PLCs at both the school and district levels. He helped Sanger Unified become one of the highest-performing districts in California's Central Valley. As an elementary and a secondary principal, Jon's schools averaged over 500 percent of the required stated academic achievement gains for the state Academic Performance Index measures.

Under his leadership, Sanger Unified schools won multiple local, state, and national awards including three National Blue Ribbon awards, fifteen California Distinguished School awards, eleven Title I Academic Achievement awards, and four National Schools to Watch awards. Jon has presented to multiple school districts throughout the United States, supporting staff implementing PLCs by sharing his expertise and practical experiences.

To learn more about Jon's work, follow @Jon_Yost on Twitter.

To book Brig Leane or Jon Yost for professional development, contact Solution Tree at pd@SolutionTree.com.

PLCs, Collaborative Teams, and Singletons

As educational consultants, we have the opportunity to work with many educators in schools throughout the United States and beyond. When Brig was working with a middle school staff, he was asked to meet with the fine arts team. The team included the band teacher (who also works at the high school), the general music teacher (who also teaches choir), the self-contained special education teacher, and a paraprofessional. Leaders had asked this group to collaborate about ways to increase student reading comprehension by increasing the amount of reading teachers expect students to do. Although each member of the fine arts team valued improving student reading, it was quickly apparent that the members' hearts were not in this work; they were only participating in the task out of a desire to comply. One team member commented that the collaborative work their leaders had assigned took away from the "real work" he felt the members needed to do for their students. The other educators agreed. Simply put, team members felt like they knew the destination the leaders expected them to get to (effective collaboration), but they had no idea how to get there.

Singletons—teachers who are the only ones at a school who teach a specific course or subject, such as the only seventh-grade mathematics teacher or the only art teacher—are often some of the most dedicated and sought-after teachers in a school. During informal conversations with students at schools in which we have worked, we find students the most excited about classes with their singleton teachers. Singletons are often very influential among staff and the community, and their excitement for their content is contagious. They can have a positive impact on school climate. Singleton teachers, such as band teachers who take students from making random noises on musical instruments to being integral parts of a group making beautiful music together, can greatly impact a healthy culture that believes all students can be successful, no matter their background or previous knowledge. Unfortunately, when leaders task singletons with the need to collaborate in schools undergoing

Professional Learning Community (PLC) at Work® transformation, they don't fit the typical configurations for collaboration; singletons don't have job-alike peers in the school with whom they can collaborate to improve achievement for all students.

Does this situation sound familiar to you? Are you a singleton or a school leader in a school that is either beginning the process of PLC transformation or already entrenched in the journey? If so, you know the architects of the PLC process, Richard DuFour, Rebecca DuFour, and Robert Eaker, outline collaboration as one of the three big ideas of a PLC.

The Three Big Ideas and Four Critical Questions of a PLC

Members of PLCs embrace three big ideas (DuFour, DuFour, Eaker, Many, & Mattos, 2016):

1. **A focus on learning:** The first (and the biggest) of the big ideas is based on the premise that *the fundamental purpose of the school is to ensure that all students learn at high levels (grade level or higher)*. This focus on and commitment to the learning of each student are the very essence of a *learning community*.

2. **A collaborative culture and collective responsibility:** The second big idea driving the PLC process is that in order to ensure all students learn at high levels, *educators must work collaboratively and take collective responsibility for the success of each student*. Working collaboratively is not optional, but instead is an expectation and requirement of employment. Subsequently, the fundamental structure of a PLC is the collaborative teams of educators whose members work *interdependently* to achieve *common goals* for which members are *mutually accountable*.

3. **A results orientation:** The third big idea that drives the work of PLCs is the need for a *results orientation*. To assess their effectiveness in helping all students learn, educators in a PLC focus on results—evidence of student learning. They then use that evidence of learning to inform and improve their professional practice and respond to individual students who need intervention or enrichment. (pp. 11–12)

One of the jobs of administrators and school leaders in a PLC is to support teachers by creating meaningful teams (DuFour et al., 2016). To develop a collaborative culture and collective responsibility, leaders must do more than put random educators together in teams and hope they collaborate about topics to positively impact student achievement. In a PLC, leaders organize educators in teams that must collectively answer the four critical questions of a PLC (DuFour et al., 2016):

1. What knowledge, skills, and dispositions should every student acquire as a result of this unit, this course, or this grade level?
2. How will we know when each student has acquired the essential knowledge and skills?
3. How will we respond when some students do not learn?
4. How will we extend the learning for students who are already proficient? (p. 36)

The task of organizing teachers in collaborative teams to answer the four critical questions is straightforward when it comes to schools with multiple teachers at any given grade level or teaching the same course. Naturally, those teachers will be able to collaborate. But what about singleton teachers? All schools have singletons, and some schools have many singletons or are made up solely of singletons.

Clear Direction for Singletons and Their Leaders

Through our work in schools, we see teachers and leaders struggling with how to appropriately organize singletons in meaningful teams and support members of singleton teams to successfully answer the four critical questions of a PLC. We wrote this book to provide clear direction on this issue for PLC leaders and singleton team members. We recommend involving and empowering singleton teachers when advancing the PLC process across a school or district, as well as for the professional development of those singleton educators who so often work in isolation.

Our goal is to make the step-by-step process for collaboration clear and more meaningful for singletons, and it is our intent to enhance singletons' motivation to collaborate as well. This book is for both singleton educators and administrators, as both must know and ensure effective implementation of the PLC process for the benefit of students. Both must also ensure structures are in place and time is available for every teacher to engage in meaningful collaboration if educators ever hope to see all students learning at high levels.

Chapter 1 seeks to bring clarity to what collaboration in a PLC looks like and how to ensure it is meaningful. Educators build key understanding of what is and isn't meaningful collaboration, and we elaborate on what actually impacts student learning. In this chapter we also describe in greater detail the singleton dilemma all schools on the PLC journey face.

Chapter 2 introduces readers to the three distinct *on-ramps* (or entry points) singletons can take to have meaningful collaboration with other educators. These on-ramps are starting points to collaboration for singletons that then guide singletons and administrators with crucial steps. These on-ramps provide choices so singletons can find the most meaningful collaboration based on their situation as they look to improve their instruction and student achievement using the PLC process.

Chapter 3 helps singletons prepare the groundwork so they are ready to collaborate in meaningful ways utilizing any of the three on-ramps. The preparation mirrors the work of a teacher on a course-alike team, but singletons will often complete this work independently. It is critical that singletons complete the work this chapter describes prior to taking any of the three on-ramps—much like a prerequisite skill needed for a class. Singletons who have completed the groundwork will be ready to engage in meaningful collaboration, but without it, singletons will lack focus and could end up concentrating their efforts in the wrong direction.

Each of the next three chapters focuses on one of the on-ramps for singletons to experience meaningful collaboration.

Chapter 4 focuses on developing teacher teams across schools, when singletons work with a course-alike singleton (or singletons) in a different school. Singletons may find one educator to collaborate with or a small group. There are benefits to any size collaborative team; the key is the educator does not work in isolation. These teams can function virtually as needed.

Chapter 5 focuses on how teachers in the same building can find meaningful collaboration by identifying common skills or concepts singletons teach in different courses. For example, some schools might only have one science teacher at the sixth-grade level and another at the seventh-grade level who don't teach common courses. These teachers could collaborate about common skills.

Chapter 6 guides teachers toward meaningful collaboration with a colleague in the same building—a critical friend—when no other teammate teaches the same skill or concept that a singleton identifies as essential.

Chapter 7 brings together the different team structures this book describes, along with the more common same-course or grade-level collaborative team structure, to ensure all teams on campus align toward meaningful collaboration leading to increased student achievement. Leaders and teams will learn ways to keep the work doable and how to work through expected resistance, and they will find checklists to guide their progress.

Included in chapters 2–6 are sections specifically for leaders and for teachers that provide short examples. In addition, chapters 4–6 include templates to guide the work of collaborative teams as they work through the four PLC critical questions.

Also included are lists of tools and resources to aid teams in their collaborative work. Throughout the book, readers will reflect on questions to consider and will take time to pause and reflect to consider both their current reality and to capture any new learning. The Perspectives From the Field segments give readers insight into how the work this book describes is impacting singleton teachers in the real world. Chapters 3–7 conclude with common reasons leaders and singleton educators might provide to not do the work. We contrast these sections with a parallel section with reasons to do the work, acknowledging that while there are significant challenges to collaborating and answering the four critical questions with fidelity, meaningful collaboration is nonetheless the right work.

A Future of Collaboration for All Educators

We fully acknowledge that the challenges in education are great; however, meaningful collaboration remains the pathway ahead for student success. We believe every educator—including singletons—should be part of a meaningful team and engage in true collaboration for the benefit of the students they serve. Students, their families, and society are counting on it.

As DuFour and colleagues (2016) write, "It is time for every educator to take *personal* responsibility for helping bring the PLC process to life in his or her school or district" (p. 262). Every educator includes singletons.

CHAPTER 1

Meaningful Collaboration

*The most valuable resource that all teachers have
is each other. Without collaboration, our growth
is limited to our own perspectives.*

—Robert John Meehan

K–12 schools and districts face daunting challenges as they strive to ensure all students learn at high levels and are prepared to be successful when they exit the school system. These challenges, such as student mobility, family trauma, and inconsistent preschool preparation, multiply as educators work with diverse student populations with a wide range of learning needs. Coupled with increased federal, state or provincial, and local accountability, schools and districts face an intensified need to eliminate the ineffective practice of educators *working in isolation*—when educators are left to themselves to determine what to teach, how to best teach it, how to assess, and how to respond to the varying needs of their students.

Most educators have had experience being part of a team at some point in their lives; maybe it was on an athletic team, in the school band, or at work, such as Jon's first job as a busboy. In Jon's team experience, the cooks prepared food and placed it on plates. The servers served the plates of food to the customers. Jon cleared the plates, washed them, and returned them to the cooks. They worked as a team. As a Coast Guard officer, Brig was part of lifesaving teams conducting dangerous rescues, and everyone on the teams played a critical role in accomplishing the mission. As the navigator, Brig would receive the distress call and direct the ship to the right location, while the driver of the rescue boat would make adjustments based on weather conditions to safely get the boat crew near enough so the rescue swimmer could jump in the water to save the person in distress. In each situation, Brig worked together with a team to accomplish a task and members depended on one another. To be successful, the members knew they had to work as a team; Jon's job as a busboy and Brig's job as a Coast Guard officer required more than any one person could do alone.

The power of teamwork has been extensively discussed and written about. Research shows organizing staff in teams that ensure frequent collaboration is a practice educators must embrace (Eaker, 2020). National Commission on Teaching and America's Future and WestEd study coauthors Kathleen Fulton and Ted Britton (2011) state:

> We now have compelling evidence that when teachers team up with their colleagues they are able to create a culture of success in schools, leading to teaching improvements and student learning gains. The clear policy and practice implication is that great teaching is a team sport. (p. 4)

According to DuFour and colleagues (2016), collaborative teams are the building blocks of a PLC. In their landmark book introducing the PLC process, Richard DuFour and Robert Eaker (1998) state, "People who engage in collaborative team learning are able to learn from one another, thus creating momentum to fuel continuous improvement" (p. 27). Coauthors Richard DuFour, Rebecca DuFour, Robert Eaker, Mike Mattos, and Anthony Muhammad (2021) share:

> A PLC is composed of collaborative teams whose members work *interdependently* to achieve *common goals*—goals linked to the purpose of learning for all—for which members hold one another *mutually accountable*. It is difficult to overstate the importance of collaborative teams in the PLC process. It is equally important, however, to emphasize that collaboration does not lead to improved results unless people focus on the right issues. Collaboration is a *means to an end*, not *the end itself*. (p. 14)

Professor of education John Hattie's (2017) research supports the importance of collaboration (as cited in Waack, 2018). In his meta-analysis, Hattie (2017) ranks 252 factors related to student achievement (as cited in Waack, 2018). The number-one influence he identifies is collective teacher efficacy (1.57 effect size—the equivalent of more than three years of academic growth in one academic year; 0.4 is considered normal academic growth; Hattie, 2017, as cited in Waack, 2018). *Collective teacher efficacy* is the belief of staff in their combined ability to positively affect student academic achievement. This further supports collaboration as favorable over teachers working in isolation; it is not the individual belief of a single staff member that positively affects student academic achievement, but rather, a staff's collective belief.

Many resources are available that outline how to implement the PLC process in your school or district. They address topics such as a guaranteed and viable curriculum (Kramer & Schuhl, 2017), common formative assessments (Bailey & Jakicic, 2017), SMART goals (strategic and specific, measurable, attainable, results oriented, and time bound; DuFour et al., 2016), response to intervention (RTI; Buffum, Mattos, & Malone, 2018), and so on.

The thread that runs through these PLC topics is collaboration: educators are more effective when they work in teams versus working in isolation, but the collaboration must be meaningful. This chapter explores what makes collaboration meaningful, the dilemma of singletons and collaboration, and common approaches for singleton collaboration.

Meaningful Collaboration Versus Collaboration Lite

It is important to define the term *meaningful collaboration* and distinguish it from what PLC resources call *collaboration lite* (DuFour et al., 2016). *Collaborate* (n.d.) comes from the Latin word *collaborare* combining *com-* and *laborare* to mean "labor together." *Collaborate* (n.d.) is also "to work jointly with others or together especially in an intellectual endeavor." However, we have learned through our experiences that a generic definition of collaboration impedes continuous improvement. Therefore, we strongly promote a narrower and more specific definition. In *Learning by Doing*, the authors specifically define *collaboration* as a "systematic process in which teachers work together interdependently in order to *impact* their classroom practice in ways that will lead to better results for their students, for their team, and for their school" (DuFour et al., 2016, p. 12). We use this definition of collaboration, as we too often observe educators misinterpreting congeniality, cooperation, and their willingness to work together as collaboration. We classify these faux interpretations as *collaboration lite*. Teams of educators who only address state standards, discipline issues, and other school issues will not see the improvement in student learning they desire. These activities do not embrace the foundational elements of the PLC process.

The significant difference between being a true collaborative team versus engaging in collaboration lite is using evidence of student learning to inform and improve both individual and collective practices. In other words, collaboration is about teams collectively analyzing their practices, most specifically their instructional practices, and seeking to discover more effective ways to help all students learn. This analysis comes from examining the evidence of learning, reflecting on instructional practices, and seeking more effective practices. This process of collectively analyzing and reflecting on practices using evidence of student learning and ultimately impacting teaching is the heart of collaboration. This process can only be done collectively when working as part of a team. If teams come together, but practices don't change as a result of their collaboration, they are participating in collaboration lite.

To help you determine if you and your collaborative teams engage in collaboration or collaboration lite, consider the examples in table 1.1.

TABLE 1.1: Examples of Collaboration Lite Versus Meaningful Collaboration

EXAMPLES OF COLLABORATION LITE	EXAMPLES OF MEANINGFUL COLLABORATION
Focusing on issues unrelated to student learning	Focusing on student learning
Sharing opinions about what works	Using evidence of student learning (work samples, exit tickets, assessment results) when seeking best practices
Being comfortable with current instructional practices and strategies	Constantly seeking better ways to improve student learning
Not using or rarely using student work in conversations about instructional practices	Bringing in evidence of student work and asking for feedback and ideas
Discussing criteria, but leaving the criteria up to individual teachers	Generating common success criteria, such as a common rubric
Discussing standards and targets, but leaving unit development up to the individual teacher	Using a protocol with specific criteria to work interdependently in planning an instructional unit

Understanding meaningful collaboration in a PLC requires an understanding of what we mean by *meaningful*. For anything to be meaningful, it must have significance. Educators must find the collaboration both valuable and worthwhile. The collaboration must make a difference and help educators accomplish goals that align with school goals. If leaders ask educators to collaborate on topics that are of little or no interest to them, or if the collaboration does not align with the mission of the school, the collaboration is nonmeaningful. For example, if leaders ask a band teacher to collaborate with other elective teachers, and the team is told to focus primarily on how to improve reading comprehension, the band teacher may eventually find the collaborative team meetings nonmeaningful. Even when the band teacher is supportive and sees the importance of all students being proficient readers, that teacher will want to eventually focus the collaboration on what she was hired to do: be the best band teacher she can be. We are not advocating for singletons to disregard schoolwide initiatives, such as increasing student aptitude in reading; rather, we advise that for collaboration to be meaningful, it should focus primarily on how it can help improve student learning for each team member's students within each team member's course or grade level.

Meaningful collaboration is about teachers collectively having the opportunity and ability to analyze their practices to discover what is most effective, as well as what is least effective. When teachers collectively engage in this analysis of their practices, they learn together, engaging in adult learning. The process of meaningful collaboration asks teachers to determine which practices have proven to increase student learning; each teacher asks, "What can I learn from my colleague to improve, and what can we all learn from one another to improve?"

Meaningful collaboration also involves creating frequent opportunities to examine evidence of student learning together (not alone) to collectively learn the impact of specific practices and strategies. Members of meaningful collaborative teams analyze practices together to *learn together*. Finally, meaningful collaboration must be about putting new learning into action. If the time teachers spend collaborating together does not lead to changes in their practices, they are not engaged in meaningful collaboration. Meaningful collaboration must lead to improvement in instructional practices and strategies that produce improved learning outcomes for students.

Remember that the *L* in PLC is for *learning*—specifically, adult learning. Collaboration is most significant when adults not only work together but also, and more importantly, when they learn together. Therefore, we define *meaningful collaboration*, adapted from the definition in *Learning by Doing* (DuFour et al., 2016), as a *significant, valuable, worthwhile*, and systematic process in which educators work together, interdependently, to analyze and impact their professional practices to improve individual and collective results. When considering singletons, we draw out a difference between collaboration and meaningful collaboration by emphasizing the imperative that the collaboration be significant, valuable, and worthwhile to the primary focus of singleton teachers. PLC experts Robert Eaker and Janel Keating (2012) contend that educators are going to work hard no matter what, but their efforts must focus on getting the best results. Now that is something to work for!

The Dilemma of Singletons

Creating meaningful collaboration is relatively simple when schools have two or more teachers teaching the exact same content. For example, creating meaningful collaboration for three seventh-grade language arts teachers is very straightforward. They teach the same curriculum, have similar students, and have the same number of days to teach the content. They can collaborate about understanding their standards, implementing effective instructional strategies, and assessing student learning in the best ways possible. A large portion of what these teachers do every day is very similar. This cannot be said of two small-school mathematics teachers, one for sixth grade and one for seventh grade, who leaders ask to collaborate. They both teach mathematics. They teach some of the same concepts. However, they also have differences. How about asking an art teacher to collaborate with a technology teacher? They both teach students. They both have to engage students in learning. But their differences are greater than their similarities. This creates a dilemma. How can singletons participate in meaningful collaboration when they don't teach the same subject, course, or grade level?

This dilemma is most prevalent in small schools, as there may be only one teacher per grade level or course. As we consider this dilemma, we will address two key questions throughout this book.

1. What can you do as a singleton teacher to create meaningful collaboration?

2. What can you do as a leader to create meaningful collaboration for singletons?

In subsequent chapters, this book explores the answers to these questions. But before that, we must explore the common approaches for singleton collaboration that are problematic.

Common Approaches for Singleton Collaboration

In our experience, leaders typically take one of three approaches for singleton collaboration. Unfortunately, these approaches attempt to fit teachers who do not teach the same content into collaborative processes designed for two or more teachers who teach the same content. The three approaches include: (1) grouping by common skills and concepts, (2) grouping by non-learning topics, and (3) grouping without guidance or direction.

Grouping by Common Skills and Concepts

The first approach is when leaders ask singleton teachers to find something in their content they have in common and collaborate about that. To accomplish this, singletons identify the common skills and concepts across their content areas and select the most meaningful ones to collaborate about. There is nothing wrong with this approach; we expand on it in chapter 5 (page 65). However, we find that if this is the primary or only focus of the collaborative team, it often produces nonmeaningful collaboration. For example, having a computer science teacher and an art teacher collaborate on the common skill of comparing and contrasting (the computer science teacher is having students compare how people work through advancements in computing technology while the art teacher is having them compare qualities of art presentation formats) is helpful. But what the computer science teacher really wants to collaborate on is how to best teach students to use technology to present data in a visual format, and the art teacher really wants to find a better way to teach art skills, such as shading. While the teachers might find their collaboration initially somewhat useful, their collaboration isn't meaningful because they aren't collaborating about the topics that will increase student and adult learning.

Grouping by Non-Learning Topics

The second approach is when leaders ask singleton teachers to collaborate about non-learning issues such as student motivation or parent communication. This grouping can have benefits—who doesn't want to learn how to best motivate students? However, if every collaborative team meeting only focuses on student motivation and the singleton art teacher wants to learn how to improve her instruction on developing the skill of mixing paints and showing color relationships, the collaboration will soon become nonmeaningful. We find that teachers desire more meaningful collaboration beyond addressing non-learning issues.

Grouping Without Guidance or Direction

The third approach leaders take is simply directing singleton teachers to meet without guidance or direction, leaving them alone and with no accountability. Leaders often take this approach not because they don't care, but because neither the leaders nor teachers know what to do. Singletons know they are supposed to collaborate, they believe in collaboration, and everyone else in the school collaborates with a team. Some singleton teachers never complain about this approach because they are left to do their own thing, and they are happy about not having to change.

Conversely, singleton teachers may feel left out and unimportant. This is especially true when they witness the successes of other collaborative teams and want the same experience for themselves.

Pause and Reflect

TEACHERS

- Does the collaboration you currently engage in lead to improved achievement in your classroom?

- How might you utilize evidence of student learning to better guide your collaboration with a teammate?

- What aspects of your current teaching assignment would you like to get a colleague's best thinking about?

LEADERS

- Have you clearly defined collaboration so your staff know why members are meeting together?

- Have you organized your singletons so they engage in collaboration they view as meaningful?

Conclusion

The question remains, How do PLC leaders create meaningful, significant collaboration for staff members who don't teach the exact same content? In the next chapter, we introduce three on-ramps that provide pathways to deepen and improve collaboration for singletons. These options provide any singleton teacher with an entry point to begin meaningful, significant collaboration with a teammate. We highlight and explain tools and resources to help you continually evolve your collaboration so it remains meaningful for all singletons. We provide guidance and templates that focus on allowing teachers to work interdependently with others. Working collaboratively is not always easy, but it is a much more powerful approach to increase student learning than working in isolation. Let's begin a meaningful collaboration journey together!

CHAPTER 2

Singleton On-Ramps for Collaboration

*If you don't know where you are going,
any road will get you there.*

**—Lewis Carroll, *Alice's Adventures
in Wonderland***

Nicole, an art teacher at Centerville High School, was somewhat frustrated. Her principal asked her to collaborate with the other elective teachers (a band teacher, a choir teacher, a Spanish teacher, a business teacher, a drama teacher, and a computer applications teacher), and that group finally did find one thing in common they could collaborate about: student presentation skills. However, what Nicole wanted to collaborate about—what was most important to her—wasn't anything she had in common with the other elective teachers. If Nicole were to be completely honest, she didn't really care that much about student presentation skills and had only collaborated out of a desire to comply. She just didn't think collaborating about improving student presentation skills would help her become a better teacher, nor would it help her students become better artists, and to put it plainly, she wasn't into it. When her principal said, "Go find something to collaborate about," she frankly thought either the principal didn't know how Nicole's elective team should collaborate when they don't share a common curriculum or the principal didn't really care.

15

Nicole felt perhaps the latter was the case since art isn't a state-tested subject. Instead, she wished she could spend her collaborative time talking about things that impact her content, such as better ways to help students learn that errors and failure are important steps in the creation of great works of art, or even how to help unmotivated art students get over the embarrassment of their rudimentary first attempts at self-portraits. Over time, her frustration was building as she could see other teams, such as the Algebra 1 team and the English 12 team, learning together, seeing increased success with struggling students, and growing in their knowledge about the topics that matter to them. Meanwhile, her team (with its focus on student presentation skills) was still trying to simply come up with an assessment aligned to the members' various courses.

Nicole's principal, Taylor, wanted to know how to transform school teams from a culture of teaching to a culture of learning. He knew how to support teachers who teach the same course, but with so many teachers teaching single courses and such a complex master schedule, he didn't know how he could find time for teachers to collaborate without asking them to give up lunch or stay after school. A union vote was required to change the master schedule, which would take at least a year. Taylor's thoughts were mixed: "I don't know where to start," "If I were to meet with my singleton teachers, I don't know what to say or how to guide them," and, "I am too busy for this."

Pause and Reflect

TEACHERS

- Is the collaboration you engage in as a singleton teacher—if any—meaningful to you and your teammates?
- How can you work with a teammate and collaborate in a meaningful way when you have very little content in common?

LEADERS

- Have you successfully organized singletons in your school or district in meaningful collaborative teams?
- What guidance and support can you provide to help singletons and other teachers learn together and become interdependent teams?

As a singleton teacher, you might have a lot in common with Nicole. As a school leader, you likely can identify with the frustration Taylor is facing. It may seem to these educators that singletons can't participate in meaningful collaboration the way course- or grade-alike teachers can. This is not true! Singletons can have meaningful collaborative team experiences. In this chapter, we present three entry points, or *on-ramps*, for collaboration that will get singletons moving forward on their PLC journey.

Singleton On-Ramps

How singletons collaborate with their colleagues can look different depending on a school's organization, staffing configuration, and other needs. We have yet to find two schools with the exact same needs. There is no one-size-fits-all approach for organizing staff in collaborative teams to create meaningful collaboration. Singleton on-ramps allow you to find your best entry into meaningful collaboration.

The term *on-ramp* refers to how to get started in meaningful collaboration. Specifically, singleton teachers use the term *on-ramp* to answer the following questions.

1. With whom should I collaborate?

2. What specific tasks should my team engage in?

3. What templates or protocols should my team utilize to guide our work?

For leaders, the term *on-ramp* answers the same questions but requires answers from a leader's perspective. The term *on-ramp* answers the following leader questions.

1. How do I help singleton teachers engage in meaningful collaboration based on their unique teaching assignment? What is the most effective way to configure the staff in collaborative teams?

2. What specific tasks should each team engage in?

3. What templates or protocols should I provide to support teams and guide their work?

To conceptualize the on-ramps for singletons, we use an analogy of traveling on a one-way road. As with any road, the condition and size of the road impact how fast one can safely and successfully travel. The same is true of the path each teacher travels on the journey of PLC transformation. The better the condition and the larger the size of the path educators travel on, the faster they can travel. Meaningful collaboration puts teachers on a faster road for improvement; they can accelerate their learning, change practices quicker, and thus improve student achievement more rapidly. Figure 2.1 shows the three singleton entry points: (1) the course-alike on-ramp, (2) the common-content on-ramp, and (3) the critical-friend on-ramp.

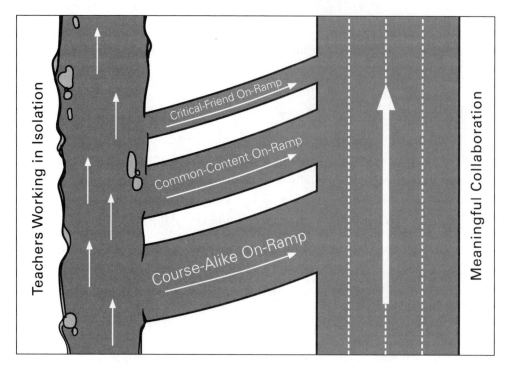

FIGURE 2.1: Singleton on-ramps for collaboration.

The far left of figure 2.1 shows teachers working in isolation on a rough road, meaning they are working under the following conditions.

- They primarily make decisions and interpretations regarding curricula, instruction, and assessment independent of anyone else.

- They make improvements to curricula, instruction, and assessment primarily on their own.

- They have limited or no ability to compare their effectiveness to others.

- They are primarily and individually responsible for self-reflecting, determining areas needing improvement, learning more effective practices, and implementing improved practices.

In some instances, districts provide a list of essential standards, a pacing guide, or assessments for teachers to utilize. When districts provide these items and ask teachers to utilize them without discussion or interaction, these teachers are working in isolation. As we explore later in the book, collaboration involves teachers interacting and learning *together* while making collective decisions, such as determining the essential learning, creating a pacing guide, and indicating the amount of instructional time teachers devote to the essential learning.

Essential learning typically comes from the standards, but it can also be dispositions the school deems essential, such as organizational skills, academic behaviors or other positive behavior–related dispositions, and social-emotional learning. Some may also refer to essential learning as *essential standards, power standards, a guaranteed and viable curriculum, essential academic goals*, or *learning expectations*. Regardless of the term, for our purposes, we are talking about those things every student should learn by the conclusion of the course or grade level.

You might ask, "Can an educator have any success working in isolation?" The answer is *yes*, but with significant limitations. An isolated teacher's success is dependent on his or her individual ability, individual learning, and ability to self-reflect and self-improve professional practices without guidance or assistance. Working in isolation limits the level of effectiveness to what a teacher can individually do to improve. Educational consultant Mike Schmoker (2006) states in *Results Now*, "Isolation is the enemy of improvement" (p. 23). Hattie (2015) expands on this point when he says:

> We must stop allowing teachers to work alone, behind closed doors and in isolation in the staffrooms and instead shift to a professional ethic that emphasizes collaboration. We need communities within and across schools that work collaboratively to diagnose what teachers need to do, plan programmes and teaching interventions and evaluate the success of the interventions. (p. 23)

Figure 2.1 depicts the three on-ramps to collaboration—the potential starting points for any teacher to begin the process of engaging in meaningful collaboration. These on-ramps are not sequential, nor are they stages. They are simply starting points to engage in meaningful collaboration. There are specific limitations to some on-ramps, and we will explain how to maximize the power of collaboration for each on-ramp.

In figure 2.1, notice the road is larger with the first on-ramp—the course-alike on-ramp—as a singleton begins to travel (collaborate) with others. This is significant because traveling on a larger road while collaborating with others who teach the same subject allows you to safely increase your rate of travel—your rate of improving your effectiveness. While not as effective as the course-alike on-ramp, the other two on-ramps are preferable to a teacher working in isolation, as their relative size in figure 2.1 indicates.

There are some commonalities between the three on-ramps. One of the most significant commonalities is a constant and continuous focus on answering the four critical questions of a PLC (DuFour et al., 2016):

1. What knowledge, skills, and dispositions should every student acquire as a result of this unit, this course, or this grade level?
2. How will we know when each student has acquired the essential knowledge and skills?
3. How will we respond when some students do not learn?
4. How will we extend the learning for students who are already proficient? (p. 36)

Answering these four critical questions must be an ongoing process. Teachers and collaborative teams continue to increase their effectiveness as they learn and clarify their collective answers to these learning-focused questions.

Since the on-ramps are not sequential nor stages, you will need to determine which on-ramp best suits your current situation. As your situation changes, your on-ramp into meaningful collaboration will also change. Each of the subsequent chapters provides the detailed guidance, tools, and protocols for both finding your on-ramps and maximizing the power of collaboration. To establish a foundation for these chapters, the following sections explore each of the three on-ramps in more detail.

Course-Alike On-Ramp

This is the most common on-ramp for collaboration in a PLC: teachers who teach the same course or content collaborate as a team. The difference for singleton teachers is that because they are the only teacher in a school who teaches a particular course, they will make a commitment to collaborating with another teacher or teachers from different schools or districts. This collaboration often takes place virtually. DuFour and colleagues (2016) call these virtual teams *electronic teams* and note that "proximity is not a prerequisite for an effective collaborative team. Teachers can use technology to create powerful partnerships with colleagues across the district, state, or world" (pp. 61–62).

For example, a singleton kindergarten teacher might collaborate with a kindergarten teacher from the other elementary school in the same district. An eighth-grade mathematics teacher might choose to collaborate virtually with another eighth-grade mathematics teacher from a different district. Collaborative teams may also consist of two or more U.S. history teachers from different states. (Note that although we do not indicate a maximum number of team members, equal participation becomes more difficult as the number of team members increases.)

For some teachers, especially in smaller schools, teaching assignments might include multiple roles—a teacher might teach the same course as someone else in the school and also be the only one teaching another course. For example, Tyler might teach English 6 and Introduction to Drama while Jordan teaches English 6, but also teaches Introduction to Robotics. Tyler and Jordan could utilize the course-alike on-ramp for English 6 and the critical-friend on-ramp for their other courses, based on their available time and capacity to do the work. In some circumstances, it might be most effective to start with one on-ramp, learn the process, and then add the second on-ramp in the future.

The course-alike on-ramp includes the following key work. (We explain this work in detail in chapter 4, page 47.)

1. Identify a colleague or colleagues to collaborate with and gain a commitment to collaborate.

2. Identify essential learning and create a common pacing guide.

3. Develop units of study for the essential learning with at least one formative assessment during the unit and another at the end of the unit.

4. Administer team-developed common formative assessments.

5. Analyze results from common formative assessments after establishing inter-rater reliability to ensure calibration of grading.

6. Design and implement interventions and extensions based on assessments.

7. Document team learning to improve practice over time.

This work by course-alike teammates allows them to answer the four critical questions of a PLC despite not working in the same building. Conceptually, think of a district with several high schools, each with one orchestra teacher, or several elementary schools, each with one music teacher. These teachers would be ideal collaborators, as districts typically share similar curricula and expectations. We address the nuances of the benefits and potential drawbacks of collaborating with other singleton teachers in the same district or with teachers from other districts in chapter 4 (page 47). While it would be great for singletons from the same district to collaborate, singletons from across a state or even across a country can collaborate; the issue is how to find those course-alike singletons. Conferences and other professional groups can be a great way to find them, as well as using the AllThingsPLC website (www.AllThingsPLC.info/Singleton) to connect to other singletons.

Common-Content On-Ramp

This on-ramp is for singleton teachers who are *not* teaching the same course or grade level but identify common skills and concepts taught in their courses; these singletons will also have skills and concepts they teach that are *not* in common. *Vertical teams*, as DuFour and colleagues (2016) describe them, "link teachers with those who teach content above and below their students" (p. 61). Teachers should utilize this on-ramp to collaboration when they (1) are the only teacher teaching a specific course or content, (2) have worked with other members of their collaborative team to identify common skills and concepts taught in their courses, *and* (3) have a commitment from those members to collaborate about this common content.

For example, two or more English teachers at a secondary school who have standards that vertically progress through the grades can use this on-ramp. A singleton fourth-grade teacher and singleton fifth-grade teacher in a small school might use this on-ramp as well. It could also be the on-ramp for two career and technical education (CTE) teachers who find they teach the same concept in their different content areas. When singletons closely examine their standards and identify the specific skills and concepts they individually teach, they typically find many commonalities that provide the basis for this on-ramp. Consider the following examples.

- A singleton U.S. history teacher has identified the following essential learning: "Students determine the central ideas or information of a primary or secondary source and provide an accurate summary that makes clear the relationships among the key details and ideas" (California Department of Education, 2000).

- A singleton world history teacher has identified the following essential learning: "Students determine the central ideas or information of a primary or secondary source and provide an accurate summary of how key events or ideas develop over the course of the text" (California Department of Education, 2000).

The singleton teachers have this essential learning in common (determine the central idea or information of a primary and secondary source), and these singletons should utilize the common-content on-ramp to collaborate.

We explain in chapter 5 (page 65) the specific steps to take to determine your on-ramp. There are key advantages to having two or more teachers collaborating on a common skill or concept taught in their individual courses, rather than using the third on-ramp, the critical-friend on-ramp. Key advantages include the ability to design common formative assessments on the exact same skill or concept and then having comparable student evidence from those same assessments.

The common-content on-ramp includes the following key work. (We explain this work in detail in chapter 5, page 65).

1. Identify a colleague or colleagues to collaborate with and gain a commitment to collaborate.

2. Examine essential learning and identify common skills and concepts.

3. Explore course pacing guides of common skills and concepts to align them to the same timeframe without jeopardizing the logical sequence of course content.

4. Collaborate to develop common formative assessments of common skills and concepts.

5. When pacing aligns, administer and collaboratively analyze results of common formative assessments.

This work by common-content teammates allows them to answer the four critical questions of a PLC despite not teaching the same course or at the same grade level.

Critical-Friend On-Ramp

Teachers may use this on-ramp when they do not have another colleague teaching the same course or content and they do not teach the same skills or concepts as other members of their collaborative team. We want to be clear: we do not consider the critical-friend on-ramp to be the most effective way to improve teacher practices, as it lacks the element of team comparison of results with the intent of identifying the most effective practices. However, we recognize that due to many different situations, sometimes teachers can only be a critical friend to a colleague, which we believe is more meaningful than leaving colleagues to work in isolation.

So what is a critical friend? Great Schools Partnership, in their online resource *Glossary of Education Reform* (2013), defines a *critical friend*:

> A critical friend is typically a colleague or other educational professional, such as a school coach, who is committed to helping an educator or school improve. A critical friend is someone who is encouraging and supportive, but who also provides honest and often candid feedback that may be uncomfortable or difficult to hear. In short, a critical friend is someone who agrees to speak truthfully, but constructively, about weaknesses, problems, and emotionally charged issues.

This on-ramp allows singletons to receive structured feedback and share effective practices with colleagues, even though the colleagues teach different grades or courses and content. This collaboration increases the learning of isolated teachers, builds their ability to critically analyze their practices, and eventually leads to changes in their practice. It supports teachers in the process of diagnosing their practices and working collaboratively with others to improve those practices. The ideal situation is collaborating with colleagues teaching the same content; however, this on-ramp allows singletons to enter into the meaningful conversations to analyze and impact practice.

DuFour and colleagues (2016) use the term *critical friends* to describe the way in which a vertical team would collaborate. Note that we are differentiating how a vertical team approaches common content versus non-common content. For example, in a vertical team consisting of a singleton second-grade teacher and a singleton third-grade teacher, the singleton second-grade teacher may have an essential learning related to money, while understanding money may not be an essential learning for the singleton third-grade teacher. In this case, the team would use the critical-friend on-ramp for the non-common content of understanding money, but use the common-content on-ramp for essential learnings they share, such as place value.

Recall the example of the U.S. history teacher and the world history teacher from the previous section. They were able to collaborate on the common content of the following standards.

- "Students determine the central ideas or information of a primary or secondary source and provide an accurate summary that makes clear the relationships among the key details and ideas" (California Department of Education, 2013a).

- "Students determine the central ideas or information of a primary or secondary source and provide an accurate summary of how key events or ideas develop over the course of the text" (California Department of Education, 2013a).

For these standards (that is, determine the central idea or information of a primary and secondary source), the teachers should utilize the common-content on-ramp for collaboration. However, if these singletons want to collaborate on the following essential standards, they should choose the critical-friend on-ramp.

- U.S. history teacher: "Students analyze America's participation in World War II" (California Department of Education, 2000).

- World history teacher: "Students trace the rise of the United States to its role as a world power in the 20th century" (California Department of Education, 2000).

In this case, the history teachers using the critical-friend on-ramp must first complete the preparation for meaningful collaboration chapter 3 (page 29) outlines. In addition, they must identify and receive a commitment from their colleague, who will act as a critical friend for collaboration and designate regular dedicated collaboration time to meet.

The critical-friend on-ramp includes the following key work. (We explain this work in detail in chapter 6, page 87.)

1. Identify and gain commitment from a colleague to act as a critical friend during frequent collaboration.

2. Gather evidence of work to share and use with a critical friend. This evidence will include determining essential learning, assessments, and intervention and extension plans. However, the focus of the shared evidence will be the evidence of student learning.

3. Use a structured protocol to self-reflect on the evidence and prepare questions for your critical friend.

4. Engage in collaborative conversations about the evidence and seek ways to improve practice.

5. Implement new learning gained through your critical-friend collaboration.

This work with a critical friend allows singletons to answer the four critical questions of a PLC despite not teaching the same course, grade level, or content.

Figure 2.2 (page 26) provides examples of situations for each on-ramp, and highlights how these entry points relate to collaborative team actions, such as improving curricula, assessment, intervention, and so on. We explore the details of these key actions for each on-ramp in more detail in chapters 4 (page 47), 5 (page 65), and 6 (page 87).

Additionally, figure 2.2 provides an overview of the three on-ramps and the situations in which singletons and school leaders should choose each. While the on-ramps and the singleton and team actions involved are clearer, you might now be wondering—like our principal (Taylor) from the beginning of this chapter—How can singleton teachers and leaders find the time for such collaborative endeavors?

Examples	Course-Alike On-Ramp Chapter 4 (This is a virtual team.)	Common-Content On-Ramp Chapter 5 (This could be a vertical team or not.)	Critical-Friend On-Ramp Chapter 6 (This could be a vertical team or not.)
1	Two Algebra 1 teachers from different schools who use the same curriculum	An industrial arts teacher and an art teacher from the same school who believe safety is essential and create a common formative assessment to measure whether students can use the personal protective equipment and operate the various machines (saws, kilns, pottery wheels, sharp instruments, and so on) proficiently	A computer teacher and an art teacher who have not identified any common content
2	Two teachers from two different campuses teaching the same course who have agreed to collaborate electronically	A seventh-grade English language arts teacher and an eighth-grade English language arts teacher from the same school who align units they are teaching so they teach a common essential standard at the same time	The only biology teacher in a school who has common collaboration time with the only band teacher
COLLABORATIVE TEAM ACTIONS			
Curriculum What are the essential knowledge, skills, and dispositions students must learn?	Determination of the essential learning and team consensus on the guaranteed and viable curriculum	Vertical teams in the same content area align the curriculum vertically, including determining rigor and progression of standards. Identification of the essential skills and concepts two or more teachers from different content areas have in common in the courses they teach	Development of a guaranteed and viable curriculum using the critical-friend protocol
Pacing How will the team determine a calendar of actions for a unit of study?	All essential learning with common pacing	For all identified common skills and concepts, team seeks to create common pacing whenever possible, but never at the expense of creating an illogical sequence of content	Independently done, with feedback from the critical-friend protocol
Assessment What type of assessments will the team use?	Common formative assessments given at the same time	Collaboration among team members to create aligned formative assessments for common skills or concepts; this may involve the creation of aligned rubrics or learning progressions. Formative assessments are common in that they are addressing the same skill or concept, but they are not identical assessments.	Individually determined formative assessments with feedback using the critical-friend protocol

Data analysis and instructional impact After the assessment, how will the team analyze data to impact instruction?	Comparison of data or student work samples from common formative assessment	Comparison of common formative assessment data and work samples aligned to rubrics to drive analysis, using an agreed-on data protocol	Partner discussion using the critical-friend protocol
Intervention How will the team respond when some students do not learn?	Team response utilizing data to drive intervention design	Team looks for opportunity to create team response by identifying common need without lowering grade-level expectancy	Individual, but discussed during the critical-friend review
SMART goals What SMART goals will the team use to measure progress?	Team SMART goal using common formative assessments	Team SMART goal using common rubric as a measurement tool	Individual SMART goal discussed during the critical-friend review

FIGURE 2.2: On-ramps with team-action examples.

The Logistics of Multiple On-Ramps

Time is one of the greatest assets for educators, but it also presents the greatest challenges. There is never enough of it; we all dream of having more time. As you determine your on-ramp (or entry point) for the most meaningful collaboration, you *must* keep this work pragmatic and doable. You must look at the collaborative work to be done and decide if it can be done within the time available. This is especially true for singleton teachers who are teaching multiple courses. You might be a teacher who has one course in common with a collaborative team member, another course where you are the only one teaching it but have identified several common concepts or skills another team member teaches, and still another course where you are the only one teaching it, but there are very few common concepts or skills other team members teach. If you determine you require multiple on-ramps for your specific teaching assignments, you might have to start with just one on-ramp. As with most things, you will become more efficient and effective over time. You may begin with the common-content on-ramp and collaborate with another teacher only about what you have in common. As time goes on and you become more efficient with collaborative processes, you may expand your collaboration and also use the critical-friend on-ramp for the content you don't have in common. Ideally, all teachers will work closely with a colleague on everything they teach. Strive for that ideal, but always keep it doable!

It is disingenuous for a leader to expect teachers to collaborate without giving them the time. Consider aligning the master schedule so teachers who share the same on-ramp have common preparation time, or working with the community to develop early release or late-start times. For other ways to find time to collaborate, refer to pages 64–67 in the third edition of *Learning by Doing* (DuFour et al., 2016).

Conclusion

This chapter introduced three on-ramps that provide pathways to deepen and improve collaboration for singletons. In the next phase of our collaboration journey together, we examine steps singletons can take in preparation for taking one of the on-ramps when a meaningful collaborative team isn't immediately available. When singletons follow the steps presented in the next chapter, they will be prepared to be a collaborative partner in the future.

Tools and Resources

Refer to these tools and resources to learn more about the content covered in this chapter.

- To learn more about different collaborative team configurations, see *Learning by Doing* (DuFour et al., 2016, pp. 60–64).

- For a more in-depth look at the four critical questions of a PLC, see *Learning by Doing* (DuFour et al., 2016, pp. 36 and 59, Here's How).

- For a reproducible tool to determine the current level of collaboration, see *Learning by Doing* (DuFour et al., 2016, p. 80, "The Professional Learning Communities at Work Continuum: Building a Collaborative Culture Through High-Performing Teams").

- For a deeper understanding of formative assessments in vertical teams, see *Simplifying Common Assessment* (Bailey & Jakicic, 2017, pp. 105–119, "Using Common Assessments With Singleton Teachers").

CHAPTER 3

Preparation for Meaningful Collaboration

*Yesterday I was clever, so I wanted
to change the world. Today I am wise,
so I am changing myself.*

—Rumi, 13th century Persian poet

When Jesse came back from summer break, it seemed like the whole culture of Orchard Mesa Middle School had changed. Ten staff members had gone to a PLC at Work Institute, and their collective outlook toward the PLC process—what had seemed like another passing fad last spring—was now gaining even more momentum. Jesse was the only computer teacher at his middle school, but the principal had told Jesse in the spring that he would need to be on a collaborative team. Since the schedule was so busy with year-end activities, Jesse was able to avoid the issue, and the time or two the principal had forced him to meet with other singletons, they were able to do a few things to appease the principal, but it didn't impact them or their classrooms in any way.

Now it was apparent that this PLC thing wasn't going away. Jesse's principal, Maya, shared some research on how teachers who work collaboratively could expect much higher levels of student learning—and the district was convinced of this as well. Jesse would simply need to find a pathway through this collaboration stuff that would make sense, but in his mind, he knew it was all a big waste of time and not nearly as important as his day-to-day teaching work and getting his students ready for the next grade level.

It was Maya's third year as a principal at Orchard Mesa—two years into its PLC journey. While the course-alike teams at Orchard Mesa were beginning to do their collaborative work well, the singletons in the building had been left out. Maya was unsure of how the singletons should begin the process of collaboration. What about the highly influential and outstanding computer teacher who has so many different classes with so many students to teach—not to mention the many extracurricular activities he is involved in? How would she find the time in the master schedule for the computer teacher to meet with another singleton on campus? And if there was time, who could the computer teacher collaborate with? Fit was a factor, as the computer teacher's curriculum was so specific it didn't have much overlap with any other teacher's curriculum.

Pause and Reflect

TEACHERS

- What could Jesse do to find meaningful collaboration?
- How could meeting with other singleton teachers be meaningful for an art teacher or a Spanish teacher or any other singleton teacher who typically works in isolation?
- What could the principal do to support singleton teachers like Jesse?

LEADERS

- If Maya can't change the master schedule right now, what are the most strategic things this principal could do to help the singleton teachers prepare for meaningful collaboration?
- What should the expectation be for singleton teachers if leaders can't yet see how they might fit into the school's collaborative journey?

In our experience working in schools, scenarios such as these are all too common. Certainly, we support leaders expecting teachers to collaborate for the benefit of students; however, when this collaboration feels forced, it is usually not meaningful.

While it would be great for every educator in a school to have a team *right now* with which to begin to answer the four critical questions of a PLC, sometimes that just isn't possible. In our work, we often encounter principals and teachers who perceive their only options related to PLC implementation to be all or nothing. Researcher, author, speaker, and consultant Jim Collins (2001) recommends that instead of choosing A *or* B, we should figure out how to have A *and* B. Some leaders might find themselves thinking, "Either these singletons collaborate with each other now, *or* they can just continue their individual work, and I will figure out the PLC process for them later." Rather than taking an all-or-nothing approach, we recommend what Collins (2001) calls the *Genius of AND* and encourage leaders to team up teachers who can be on course-alike teams *and* work differently with isolated singletons who don't have a meaningful team yet. Perhaps the singletons don't have time in the master schedule to collaborate, or there isn't enough overlap of essential skills to make the collaboration meaningful. In these situations, leaders can still make sure the building blocks for *future* successful collaboration are set. This entails singletons having (1) clarity on what is essential in each course, (2) ways to assess if students have learned the essential skills, and (3) pacing to fit the essential learning into the school year.

Singleton Responsibilities in Preparation for Meaningful Collaboration

Our message to singletons who don't yet have a partner or team is this: *you have work to do, even if you have to begin that work in isolation.* As a follow-up to the quote that opens this chapter, sometimes the only one you can change is yourself:

> It is time for our profession to become wise. It is time to stop waiting for others. It is time for every educator to take **personal** responsibility for helping bring the PLC process to life in his or her school or district. (DuFour et al., 2016, p. 262)

Answer the following questions to help determine if a singleton could best accomplish the preparatory steps (we explain in the forthcoming sections) individually or if an opportunity exists for the singleton to find a collaborative team partner now.

- Is there another teacher *in the same building* who teaches the same subject and grade level and is willing and able to collaborate? If *yes*, this work should be done with a collaborative partner. If *no*, this work should be done individually. (Note that in a PLC, collaboration should be a schoolwide expectation, and not left to each individual teacher's discretion.)

- Is there another teacher *in another building or another district* who teaches the same subject and grade level who is looking for a meaningful collaborative partner? If *yes*, this work should be done with that collaborative partner electronically. If *no*, this work should be done individually.

- Is there common time *during the workday* on a consistent basis to collaborate with another singleton teacher? If *yes*, complete the steps in this chapter, and then proceed to collaborate with another singleton teacher using the critical-friend process (see chapter 6, page 87). If *no*, completing the preparation work this chapter describes will help with readiness for future meaningful collaboration.

For isolated singleton teachers to be ready to collaborate in a meaningful way, they must do the following.

1. Know the required or essential learning in their courses.

2. Have at least one formative assessment for each essential learning to measure student learning.

3. Know the pacing of the essential learning throughout the unit and school year.

Teachers who complete these required steps will be ready to collaborate, and teacher clarity on those essential learnings will benefit current students. Teachers attempting to collaborate without completing these required steps would most likely be simply sharing opinions and ideas; without specific essential learning, ways to assess that learning, and curriculum pacing, future collaboration will be less meaningful.

Preparation Step 1: Determining the Essential Learning

If a singleton teacher has yet to develop meaningful collaboration with another teacher or team, the singleton must still answer the four critical questions of a PLC to set the groundwork for future collaboration. To determine the essential learning of their courses, singletons need to take personal responsibility for answering the first PLC critical question, "What knowledge, skills, and dispositions should every student acquire as a result of this unit, this course, or this grade level?" (DuFour et al., 2016, p. 36). In chapter 4 of *Professional Learning Communities at Work and High Reliability Schools*, National Board Certified teacher William M. Ferriter states that a critical first step for schools is to prioritize the concepts and skills that matter most (Eaker & Marzano, 2020).

If a school has a mission of high levels of learning for all—as we believe it should—teachers in every classroom must be clear on exactly what students are to learn as a result of each unit. The list of these essential learnings can't be too long. As Mattos and colleagues (2016) recommend, teacher teams should "identify eight to ten essential standards per subject, per semester" (p. 79), otherwise teachers will not have time to track student learning and intervene as needed. This is the guaranteed and viable curriculum researchers Robert Eaker and Robert J. Marzano (2020) identify. *Guaranteed* means the teacher will teach the essential content, with students receiving targeted interventions on essential learnings if they don't learn them during initial instruction. The curriculum is *viable* when teachers can teach the number of essential standards and intervene (when necessary) in the time available.

While states or districts may assist in the process or even narrow the standards, teachers are the ones who must determine the essential learning. Although essential learning comes from national, state or provincial, or local standards, everything in the standards cannot be essential, as some learning is simply more important than the rest, and the volume of standards makes treating all of them as essential implausible. Teachers must ensure all students *learn* all the essentials, while teachers need only *teach* the rest of the curriculum. This requires prioritization of the standards, and teachers must be involved in that process.

In his book *The Seven Habits of Highly Effective People*, author Stephen R. Covey (1989) only once states that the reader should mark a phrase down, asterisk it, circle it, and underline it. He does this for the phrase, "Without involvement, there is no commitment" (Covey, 1989, p. 143). If the teacher the leader expects to teach the essential learning, assess it, and intervene and extend it is not personally involved in determining exactly what students are to know and be able to do, the teacher will be less committed to ensuring all students learn it. As coauthors Anthony Muhammad and Luis F. Cruz (2019) state, "People are less likely to tear down a fence they help build" (p. 70). This does not mean teachers shouldn't teach nonessential standards. Teachers can still cover them, and some students will learn them, but some won't. Grades for those nonessentials can go in the gradebook, and teachers will move on after teaching them. Teachers don't have time to intervene on everything they teach, but it is critical they do so for the essential learning.

In a unit of study, teachers must know which learning is essential for students to know and be able to do, which learning is nice for students to know, and if teachers may have to sacrifice any of the learning due to time constraints. We recommend using the *REAL criteria* to help teachers in the selection of essential learning (Many & Horrell, 2014). Essential learning meets most, if not all, of these criteria.

- **Readiness:** Does the learning develop student readiness for the next level of learning? Is it essential for success in the next unit, course, or grade level?

- **Endurance:** Does the learning have endurance? Do teachers expect students to retain the knowledge and skills over time as opposed to merely learning it for a test?

- **Assessed:** Do teachers assess the learning? Will teachers cover the learning on state testing or college entrance, military, or trade school tests?

- **Leverage:** Does the learning have leverage? Will proficiency in this standard help students in other areas of the curriculum and academic disciplines?

Once teachers use the REAL criteria to prioritize the standards, the essential learning must be unpacked. Many resources aid educators in the process of *unpacking* (also known as *unwrapping*) standards into learning targets to then identify the essential learning that will become the guaranteed and viable curriculum. *School Improvement for All* by PLC experts Sharon V. Kramer and Sarah Schuhl (2017) contains a very effective description of the steps to this process.

Simply put, teachers who take standards through the unpacking process will be much more familiar with the standards, will have a better understanding of the rigor the standards expect, and will be able to divide each standard into several specific learning targets. The process helps teachers identify the vocabulary students will need to become familiar with to be proficient in the standard, and teachers will be better prepared to help students know the relevance of the standard. Figure 3.1 is a template teachers can use to simplify the unpacking process. Start with a standard and work to grow your knowledge of the standard. Then, prepare to take essential learning through the PLC process.

To assist singletons in gaining clarity on how to identify essential learning, see figure 3.2 (page 36). While there are many templates that isolated singletons could use to guide their thinking about the essentials in their classes, the template in figure 3.2 is simple and easy to use when not collaborating as part of a team. It is primarily a graphic organizer to help a teacher categorize the curriculum in an upcoming unit into three parts: (1) the essential learning in the unit of study that every student must learn, even if it takes multiple attempts, (2) the learning that is nice to know, which could be taught to students who have already demonstrated their learning of the essentials on an assessment, and (3) the parts of the curriculum that there isn't time to cover, and therefore teachers must sacrifice these parts of the curriculum to ensure students have ample opportunities to demonstrate their learning of the essentials.

The concept of *backward design*—of having clarity on exactly what students are to learn as a starting point—just makes sense. Consider the example of a road trip. When taking a road trip, before deciding on anything else, you must first know the

Standard		
Content (Nouns) **What Students Need to Know**	Skills (Verbs) **What Students Need to Be Able to Do**	DOK
Student Learning Targets		

Source: Kramer & Schuhl, 2017, p. 71.

FIGURE 3.1: Unpacking template.

*Visit **go.SolutionTree.com/PLCbooks** to download a reproducible version of this figure.*

destination. The same concept applies to the classroom, as coauthors Jay McTighe and Grant Wiggins (2004) explain in their definition of *backward design*:

> In backward design, one starts with the end—the desired results (goals or standards)—and identifies the evidence necessary to determine that the results have been achieved, that is, the assessments. With the results and assessments clearly specified, one can determine the necessary (enabling) knowledge and skill, and the teaching needed to equip students to perform. (p. 290)

Research supports the importance of all teachers having clarity on what they expect students to know and be able to do—the guaranteed and viable curriculum—and while it is best to do that work with colleagues (DuFour et al., 2016; Marzano, 2003), leaders should still expect this clarity from those teachers working in isolation who are preparing to be effective collaborative partners.

This step may be difficult or feel overwhelming for an isolated singleton to complete. Instead of thinking about the whole year of essential learning, teachers can divide the work into smaller chunks. The first chunk would be to ask yourself, "What does every student need to know and be able to do in the next few weeks?" Leaders can ask the same questions of their singleton teachers one unit at a time, as they encourage their staff to make the shift from trying to teach everything to ensuring that every student learns everything teachers determine essential.

Identifying Essential Learning for Singletons—Preparation for Meaningful Collaboration

Unit: _____

Date: _____

Before the Unit Begins

Instructions: Complete this form prior to starting the unit to identify essential learning. This process involves unpacking standards into essential learning targets. Each essential learning target (which answers critical question one) should go through critical questions two, three, and four of the PLC process.

Guiding questions for educators to consider (REAL criteria):

1. **Does the learning develop student readiness for the next level of learning?** Is it essential for success in the next unit, course, or grade level?

2. **Does the learning have endurance?** Do teachers expect students to retain the knowledge and skills over time as opposed to merely learning them for a test?

3. **Do teachers assess the learning?** Will the essential learning be on state tests or college entrance, military, or trade school tests?

4. **Does the learning have leverage?** Will proficiency in the standard help students in other areas of the curriculum and other academic disciplines?

Resources to assist in making decisions:

- National, state or provincial, or local standards

- Unified district curricula

- Former lesson plans (what teachers taught versus what they intended to teach)

- State test samples

- Unit books

- Item analysis

- Prerequisite skills for the next course or grade level essential for success at that level

Learning that is essential for students to know and be able to do in this unit (not more than ten essentials per half year):

Learning that is nice to know (this section is good material for extensions):

Learning teachers can sacrifice:

Source: REAL criteria adapted from Many & Horrell, 2014. Copyright © 2021 by Brig Leane. Used with permission.

FIGURE 3.2: Identifying essential learning for singletons—Preparation for meaningful collaboration.

*Visit **go.SolutionTree.com/PLCbooks** to download a reproducible version of this figure.*

Preparation Step 2: Creating a Formative Assessment for the Essential Learning

Once a singleton teacher compiles a list of the essential learning, they need to have a way to formatively assess each essential learning. This does not need to look like a large end-of-unit assessment; it can instead be a short, focused assessment teachers use to determine whether students have mastered the essential learning. This assessment creates actionable data and is known as *formative assessment* because the results inform instruction (Bailey & Jakicic, 2017). The assessment could be an exit ticket or a quiz, but it could be just a few questions or even a project or an observation. There are many resources to assist teachers with writing quality assessments, but the rigor of the assessment must be at the rigor level teachers require for students to be proficient at grade level on other end-of-year assessments. The teacher might generate an assessment question, or it might come from a textbook. Regardless of the source, the teacher should identify or create an actionable assessment; the teacher must be able to sort student results into those who are proficient and those who are not yet proficient.

This step might challenge educators who doubt their ability to write an effective formative assessment. Educators can ask themselves questions such as, "What could the students produce that would indicate to me that they are proficient on this essential learning?" "Would the assessment I am considering allow me to quickly put students into two groups—those who have learned the essential learning and those who have not?"

Leaders can support teachers by ensuring they receive training about rigor and depth of knowledge and know the formative assessments they design are not chiseled in stone, but will instead be revised and improved over time as part of the ongoing PLC process.

Preparation Step 3: Pacing of the Essential Learning

Once singleton teachers determine the essential learning and the corresponding formative assessments, they are ready to determine where the essentials and formative assessments will fit into the school year. Some teachers will not be ready to identify all the essentials and assessments for an entire year before beginning this process. Those teachers can begin by developing the essentials and formative assessments for an upcoming unit, as well as a calendar of when the unit will begin, end, and when they will give the formative assessment (we recommend somewhere in the middle of the unit). Since singletons have already built the units, they can later assemble them into a yearlong plan of all the essential learning. An example of a year-at-a-glance of essential learning for a seventh-grade mathematics teacher appears in figure 3.3 (page 38).

1	Essential learning	Use proportional relationships to solve multistep ratio and percent problems.
	Common formative assessment date	October 30; retake November 12–17
	Data preparation	November 2
2	Essential learning	Solve real-world and mathematical problems involving the four operations with rational numbers.
	Common formative assessment date	December 3; retake December 14
	Data preparation	December 7
3	Essential learning	Use variables to represent quantities in a real-world or mathematical problem, and construct simple equations and inequalities to solve problems by reasoning about the quantities.
	Common formative assessment date	January 8; retake January 19
	Data preparation	January 11
4	Essential learning	Solve real-life and mathematical problems involving angle measure, area, surface area, and volume.
	Common formative assessment date	January 27; retake February 7
	Data preparation	February 1
5	Essential learning	Use random sampling to draw inferences about a population.
	Common formative assessment date	March 3; retake March 15
	Data preparation	March 8
6	Essential learning	Investigate chance processes and develop, use, and evaluate probability models.
	Common formative assessment date	March 25; retake April 3
	Data preparation	March 28
7	Essential learning	Use appropriate tools strategically.
	Common formative assessment date	April 13; retake May 2
	Data preparation	April 16

FIGURE 3.3: Seventh-grade mathematics essential learning year-at-a-glance example.

Putting essential learning and dates in a list or on a calendar can feel very confining. Educators should remember that the dates are guidelines they should follow as closely as possible; there can be some flexibility if, for example, unexpected situations like a fire drill disrupt class. However, following the calendar plan closely is necessary to ensure the steps in the PLC process happen.

Leaders should expect teachers to know the date for each step in the PLC process. This is made easier when leaders provide teachers with calendars that include schoolwide events such as days off, assemblies, or testing windows, so teachers can plan more effectively.

The intent of developing this list or calendar is to ensure these three required steps are in place for singleton teachers who don't yet have a meaningful collaborative partner. While this is the right place to start, it is not the final destination—just a reasonable and important starting point.

Pause and Reflect

TEACHERS

- How are these steps similar to and different from your experience as a singleton teacher in your school or situation?

- In what ways do your students and you benefit if you complete the three preparation steps: (1) know the essential learning required, (2) have at least one formative assessment for each essential learning, and (3) know the pacing of the essential learning throughout the unit and school year?

- What next steps are you considering to better prepare yourself for future collaboration with another singleton?

LEADERS

- What are some effective ways to help singleton teachers make the shift from trying to teach everything to ensuring learning of the essentials?

- What next steps are you considering to help singleton teachers make a plan for how to determine the essential learning, plan for formative assessment, and pace the steps to the PLC process?

After working through the three preparation steps, some singletons will want to go even further with some additional steps to enhance their preparation for future collaboration and benefit their current students. We recommend those singletons set SMART goals for the percentage of students who will be proficient on each of the essential learnings they identify, develop an intervention and extension plan for students immediately following each formative assessment, and reflect after each unit about what they learned about their instruction as a result of this process (DuFour et al., 2016). Teachers should set SMART goals they look to improve on year after year, as their experience grows and they incorporate meaningful collaboration into their work. The SMART goals singletons set will be the same as those educators working in teams, except singletons will describe the goal for *their* students (rather than *all* students across a team). For example, a singleton eighth-grade mathematics teacher working in isolation could have a SMART goal that states, "Eighty-two percent of *my* eighth graders will be proficient at solving two-step equations from a word problem by October 8" rather than "Eighty-two percent of *all* eighth graders will be proficient at solving two-step equations from a word problem by October 8."

Intervention and extension also differ from a traditional collaborative team because the classroom singleton teacher handles those steps, rather than team members across classrooms. While the singleton teacher is preparing to be a good collaborative partner, the needs of students who haven't demonstrated their learning on the essentials will become evident. Until the singleton teacher finds a meaningful partner, the singleton teacher must handle intervention and extension planning alone for the essential learnings.

Pause and Reflect

TEACHERS

- Are you setting SMART goals, planning and carrying out interventions and extensions after you have formative assessment data, and reflecting on your practices in your classes?

- Are you making it clear to students what you expect them to learn?

- Are students who struggle with essential learning getting timely support?

- Considering that isolation is the enemy of improvement, what are your plans to find ways to collaborate?

- What next steps are you considering?

Perspectives From the Field

As a teacher who moved from working with a strong middle school mathematics team with well-established essential skills, I felt I had the ability to take my knowledge and experience and help students by defining essential skills as a singleton in my own elementary mathematics intervention classroom, where I am now a team of one. In defining the essential skill of counting from one to twenty with one of my kindergarten students, he (Johnny) realized the importance of what we were working on each day he entered my intervention classroom, and that I believed he could reach his goal. Johnny could talk about his goal and knew we would work on it until he could demonstrate mastery to both of us. He soon was able to tell others, with pride, what skill he had learned when he met his goal. Just remember students need to understand each essential skill and its importance and how it will benefit them in their education.

Keeping each grade-level list of essential skills as a mathematics interventionist allows me to share those skills with students at each grade level, which helps teachers adjust to the mathematics skills students are coming with or not coming with from year to year. I hope to see students advancing with higher levels of knowledge because I was able to catch the areas they were weak in and fix them immediately. If you miss out on learning or accomplishing an essential skill, it will show when students move on to the next grade. Until I find another mathematics interventionist to collaborate with, I am making a big difference with students as I clarify what they have to learn.

—Leslie H., singleton intervention teacher

A Note for Leaders: Providing Support and Tracking PLC Products

When leaders ask singletons to collaborate without clarity on what to collaborate about and how to do it, the collaboration is often ineffective. Teachers become frustrated, and some become negative influences on schoolwide PLC implementation. This can undermine an often-fragile PLC process in its infancy on a campus.

For example, in one school Brig worked in, the principal and several teachers had begun to implement the PLC process on site. Unfortunately, the leaders simply told elective teachers in the school to become a team and find something to collaborate about. The team was not given much guidance, but the leaders expected them to meet every week. One singleton teacher found the work to be a waste of time and openly shared that opinion in staff meetings and around the district, significantly undermining teacher buy-in.

Leaders should proceed by helping all singletons identify their best on-ramp (entry point), even if the on-ramp is not yet available. Leaders should support singletons as they begin the preparation work on their own. This often involves sitting with isolated singletons and working through the preparatory steps with them.

After introducing the PLC process and its expectations and products, leaders must know which teachers and teams need additional assistance. As Mattos and colleagues (2016) mention in *Concise Answers to Frequently Asked Questions About Professional Learning Communities at Work*, "We have found that the best approach is for principals and team leaders to agree on the work to be done, establish a timeline for completion, and clarify the evidence that teams will present to demonstrate their work" (p. 59). The knowledge leaders gain when they monitor this evidence helps them know which teachers or teams need more time and support. We will discuss this in greater detail in chapter 7 (page 103), and share an example of a spreadsheet that allows any singleton teacher to examine any other teacher or team's PLC products. This shared spreadsheet improves clarity of expectations, measures progress, shows examples for celebrations, and helps foster a culture of positive peer pressure for teachers to know and do the work leaders expect.

Some teachers may not know how to proceed in determining the essential learning in a unit of study. In these cases, templates and protocols, such as those in figure 3.1 (page 35), can help guide teachers as they are learning how to take this step. In *Leading With Intention* (2019), PLC process veterans Jeanne Spiller and Karen Power state, "Protocols are effective because by simply following the steps, the team stays focused on the right work" (p. 28). Simply put, leaders need to give guidance to teachers for what they expect them to do, and templates can be very effective for this purpose.

While the specific templates teachers should use to ensure completion of the PLC processes are optional, expecting some products to account for the work shouldn't be. Leaders should not only teach their singleton staff members about the expected PLC products but also give frequent feedback on and track those products to see which teachers need more time and support. If leaders do not inspect what they expect, they break a basic management philosophy and send the message that the work really isn't that important. To be clear, the *products* are artifacts, such as listings of essential learnings, SMART goals for student proficiency on those essential learnings, common formative assessments, student learning results, intervention and extension plans, and reflections regarding what teachers are learning through the PLC process to improve their practice.

As teachers learn the preparation steps, leaders should share and display exemplary team products so teachers can learn from one another what the leaders expect and celebrate progress. This applies to sharing singleton products as well as team products. If singleton teachers are unable to complete the work leaders expect, the leaders should consider the following reasons.

1. The teachers don't understand why the leaders expect them to complete the work.

2. The teachers don't know how to use the templates to do the work.

3. The teachers don't have the time or support to meet the expectation.

If any of these reasons are valid, leaders should meet with each singleton to understand the reason the work is not being completed and resolve the lack of understanding.

Pause and Reflect

LEADERS

- In what ways could you make the expectation of collaborative team products known to all of your teachers?

- In what ways could you provide meaningful feedback to teachers who have submitted their collaborative team products and inspect what you expect?

- When thinking about providing great examples of teacher work for others to emulate, in what ways could you celebrate those great examples?

Why Do It? Preparation

In our work in schools, we hear many reasons—or, more accurately, excuses—singleton teachers and leaders may have for not wanting to do the work of collaboration. The following list reveals the reasons we often hear about why not to do the work; a list of counter reasons why we know this work is vital follows. Which of the reasons in these lists resonate with you?

- **Reasons to Not Do the Work**
  - "It's too time-consuming to sift through all the standards to determine what is most important and what is least important."

▸ "I have always taught the chapter or unit, tested students, recorded the grades, and moved on to the next chapter and lesson. That works for my students."

▸ "Looking at data could be embarrassing for teachers. Some students just can't seem to learn the essentials, and that reflects poorly on the teacher and the school."

▸ "Doing this work takes too much time. It's just not possible."

▸ "Our overall school achievement is good enough. Why change something that isn't broken?"

▸ "If we call something *essential,* it feels like educators are responsible for every student to learn it, even if students can't or won't. That's too much responsibility."

▸ "It is too difficult to narrow down the learning to one skill or bit of essential knowledge in a unit."

▸ "There are too many curricula to cover."

We acknowledge that these reasons come up frequently and are real, especially that there are too many curricula to cover. We encourage leaders to contrast the concept of teaching everything with the idea of ensuring the learning of the essentials to remind teachers they don't have to intervene with everything students don't learn—just the essential learning.

- **Reasons to Do the Work**

    ▸ Getting clarity as singleton teachers on what is essential for students to learn helps teachers and students know what is most important.

    ▸ When students know the essentials and know where they are in learning those essentials, learning becomes more relevant and the responsibility for learning becomes shared between the stakeholders.

    ▸ The work of determining essential learning with another colleague in the future is already started, making future meaningful collaboration more productive.

    ▸ If external factors force temporary school closures, teachers who have already determined essential curricula from nice-to-know learning are much more prepared to ensure learning of essential standards is still happening.

    ▸ Organizations that don't improve and evolve over time will soon become obsolete and unable to compete.

▶ Without this work being completed in classes, targets will be unclear to students, interventions and extensions will be unfocused, parents will be of limited assistance in the learning process, and the groundwork for future collaborative teaming won't have been done.

▶ Students are more likely to hit targets if they know what the targets are.

▶ Teachers with clarity on what they expect students to learn have much more focused activities and assessments.

▶ Students who do not learn the first time gain hope that their teacher has not given up on them.

Conclusion

Sometimes for a singleton, a meaningful collaborative team just isn't immediately available. Instead of thinking the whole PLC process must wait until a team is available, or worse, putting a team together that isn't meaningful, singletons who follow the steps from this chapter will impact current students and prepare to be a great collaborative partner in the future. In the next chapter, we examine the first and most powerful on-ramp for singletons to find meaningful collaboration: the course-alike on-ramp—the virtual team.

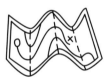

Tools and Resources

Refer to these tools and resources to learn more about the content covered in this chapter.

For instructions on how to help teachers and teams develop clarity on what all students must know and be able to do, including unpacking standards, pacing of the calendar, and so on, see the following resources.

- *Learning by Doing* (DuFour et al., 2016, pp. 112–121)

- *School Improvement for All* (Kramer & Schuhl, 2017, pp. 58–63)

- *Simplifying Common Assessment* (Bailey & Jakicic, 2017, pp. 21–26)

CHAPTER 4

Course-Alike On-Ramp: The Virtual Team

The traditional work of a collaborative team is not bound by location. Using modern tools for communication, teams can meet via video conferencing, share documents, and engage in the same conversations they would have if the meetings were taking place face to face.

—Aaron Hansen

Maria had never had an interview like the one she just left at Howell High School. It wasn't just with the principal; it had been with several members of the elective-teacher team and two teachers from nearby high schools who teach drama, the same subject Maria was applying to teach at Howell. They asked Maria questions about specific instances when a colleague deeply influenced her instruction, the percentage of students Maria felt was acceptable *not* learning an essential standard, and other questions, indicating not only was student learning foundational to this school and team but also there was the expectation that teachers would be learning from one another.

The teachers from other schools shared with Maria the team norms they used for their electronic collaborative team. They were not the standard norms, such as "Show up to online meetings on time," "Be nice," or "No online shopping during team meetings." This team had norms that really spelled out the commitments teachers had made to one another. One norm stood out: "Within two days of giving a common formative assessment, the team will have developed an action plan for students who have and have not learned the essential standard." While Maria did feel the tightness of this norm (it applied equally to all, without caveats), she could see this team was planning for what teachers know in their hearts happens after giving an assessment: some students learned it and some didn't. Maria only hoped the school would call her in for a second interview, or better yet, learn she had the job at this school, on this unique team.

Antoine was stuck. He knew as a principal how important it is for teachers to have meaningful collaboration, and he wanted to find that for Janelle, his family and consumer science (FACS) teacher, the only FACS teacher in the high school. The troubling point was that the FACS teacher was very influential and an outstanding teacher on campus who was also married to a board member. If Antoine asked Janelle to do something that seemed like a waste of time to her, it could be very detrimental to the overall PLC process in the school. He had seen the power of collaboration; his singleton drama teacher had become part of an effective team before resigning last month to relocate to a different state. He wanted to support Janelle in finding a similar situation for teaming.

Pause and Reflect

TEACHERS

- In what ways does your school prioritize the big idea of collaboration, even for singletons?
- In what ways does resistance to collaboration negatively impact your school's PLC transformation efforts?

LEADERS

- If an administrator doesn't have course-alike teachers at the same school, in what ways could the administrator encourage each educator to reach out to find educators in other schools who teach the same courses?
- Do you support singletons by sharing with them what teacher networks are available?

Maria's experience in her interview at Antoine's school shows what is possible with course-alike collaboration. This chapter explores the power of course-alike collaboration and required commitments of course-alike teammates, and provides guidance for virtual teams. The PLC Critical Questions on a Course-Alike Team section (page 53) describes how such a team collaborates, and the chapter ends with notes for leaders and reasons to do the work.

The Power of Course-Alike Collaboration

The most effective team configuration in a PLC is teams whose members are teachers of the same course or grade level, such as four second-grade teachers or three teachers of English 10 who share a common curriculum. These teachers can most easily collaborate about the four critical questions of a PLC.

For singletons who don't have a same-subject teacher in the building, the most meaningful collaboration will come with finding a same-subject teacher in another building in the same district, in a neighboring district, in the state or province, or anywhere around the globe. From our experience, the closer the better, with teachers from the same district being the best for collaboration, followed by those in the same state or province, as those teams have more aligned expectations and state standards, making collaboration easier. The challenge can sometimes be how to find these colleagues. Teachers and leaders can develop meaningful teams for singletons through social media professional learning network groups; statewide initiatives to connect singletons (such as the Arkansas Department of Education has); or at conferences on specific subjects and where singletons can meet other same-subject teachers. These connections might also be made in larger districts with multiple singleton teachers across campuses.

When singleton teachers connect electronically, there will most likely be a need for adjustments to the PLC process. For example, while some singleton team members' essential standards might align perfectly, others will not. Because of this, singletons in different schools might be unable to give a common formative assessment on the same day. This means that, at times, the team may have to delay some of the PLC process discussions about critical questions three and four until both partners have had time for their students to take the common formative assessment. In situations such as this, the team can still discuss strategies for intervention and extension, even if those action steps are not carried out at the same time. Leaders can help facilitate the work by being patient with virtual teams and finding ways to find the time teachers need to align collaboration times with their virtual colleagues.

Perspectives From the Field

As a singleton in a school implementing the PLC process, I felt as if the process wasn't designed with me in mind, and the content I taught was not compatible with the requirements. After further coaching and some thought, I found the process could work if I tried it with other elective teachers in the district. I thought that would certainly be more beneficial than trying to work in isolation. I came in contact with the theater teacher from a neighboring district. She taught the same classes as me, so why weren't we doing this together all along?

With the technology of video conferencing part of everyday life after COVID-19, we were able to meet semiregularly without even having a formal common planning period. (There is conversation happening this year to get us a scheduled meeting time!) We are able to write assessments together, share curricula, and improve our own lessons based on our findings during our checks for inter-rater reliability. It was everything I heard PLC was supposed to be, and it was well worth the investment of time and effort to reach across district lines and feel supported by someone in my niche content area.

Singletons, especially performing arts singletons, I hear you. This process at a whole-staff level can sound frustrating and nonapplicable. My experience has made me a believer in the PLC process and helped me become a stronger and more accountable educator.

—Kaitlin P., singleton performing arts teacher

Required Commitments of a Course-Alike Teammate

Teachers who are willing to collaborate electronically must be willing to commit to the PLC process with their partner (or partners). This includes planning to give their time and focused efforts on the work of the team within each unit of study, including the following.

- Defining the essential learning
- Setting a SMART goal for the essential learning
- Creating a common formative assessment to measure mastery of the essential learning
- Establishing inter-rater reliability by grading several assessments alone and then sharing grades after each assessment and discussing reasons for the grades

- Sharing and analyzing comparative data from the team-developed common formative assessments to learn together and identify the most effective instructional practices

- Developing an action plan for students who have and have not learned

- Capturing teacher learning for continuous instructional improvement

When the singleton team works through these critical steps, it creates a guaranteed and viable curriculum. If the team is new and can only work through this process eight times a year, then those eight essential learnings become the guaranteed and viable curriculum. Teachers teach many other concepts and skills, but on those eight essential learnings, the team guarantees that teachers will intervene and extend the learning. (Those other areas might overlap with the virtual teammate or teammates.) For team members experienced at this process, the maximum number of recommended essentials a team should have in a school year is twenty, with ten to twelve being more likely for teams very proficient at the process. Twelve essentials in a thirty-six week school year equate to working through the process approximately every three weeks. Note that this is a guide; some teams will have more, some less.

Once you identify and receive a commitment from one or more teammates who teach the same course, you will need to discuss and agree on some key logistical issues. Use figure 4.1 (page 52) to capture team commitments.

The key to working collaboratively and maintaining strong working relationships is making collective, not individual, decisions on all key questions facing the team.

Some teams, when answering the questions in figure 4.1, will find they need to meet virtually before or after school, and if they live near one another, meet at a central location, such as a coffee shop on in-service or other days or times when leaders expect teachers to collaborate. Shared Google documents are a great way for virtual teams to share agendas, team decisions, team products, next steps, and norms.

Team norms for virtual teams are just as important as they are for traditional teams. Effective teams will have norms that address issues that, if unaddressed, can detract from team effectiveness. Consider team norm statements that address potential questions such as, "How often will we meet? What are our starting and stopping times? What does active participation look and sound like?" Norms can address expectations for interaction with other team members such as being prepared for meetings, looking for ways to celebrate the work, using technology only to support the process, following written agendas, and handling differing opinions. Virtual teams might also consider how soon they will create unit common formative

---

Team: _____

Members: _____

- How often will we collaborate? (Recommend weekly.)

- What time will we collaborate and for how long? (Recommend a minimum of forty-five minutes weekly.)

- How will we store and share documents, such as team-developed assessments?

- Will the products we create be available to each team member's administrator?

- What virtual platform will we use to meet together?

- What process will we take to determine what we will be collaborating about each week? (Recommend using an agenda.)

- Do team members each have a commitment from their administrator allowing them to meet at the agreed-on time?

- Since team members work in different buildings, what is the expectation for communicating regarding interruptions or obstacles to fulfilling our agreements to one another? For example, what if one member is ill? Do we move the meeting or cancel it?

FIGURE 4.1: Course-alike team commitments form.
Visit go.SolutionTree.com/PLCbooks to download a reproducible version of this figure.

assessments, how soon after common formative assessments teachers will grade them, how many common formative assessments will be co-graded to ensure inter-rater reliability, how long after the assessment team members will compare results, and how long after comparing results they will implement a plan for intervention and extension. Teams that take time to spell out norms to guide collaboration will do much better when inevitable issues arise.

Guidance for Virtual Teams

If your virtual team is unclear on exactly how to work through the PLC process, perhaps members need some guidance. Using the templates in this chapter can be very helpful road maps for those teams not quite sure how to do the work. And while templates can guide critical team discussions, the growth of students and educators is the goal—not filling out the templates. Discussions and learning with colleagues and seeking outside assistance when no one on the team is getting results—these are what lead a team toward collective teacher efficacy, which doesn't happen overnight. It isn't a "microwave" situation—it's more of a "slow cooker." Outside assistance includes the team seeking input from a district content specialist, or the team doing research on ways to address a common struggle through books, videos, or other resources. Some district leaders might be unable to assist the virtual partner in the other district, but they should be able to assist the virtual partner in their district.

It is easy for teachers from different schools who teach the same subject to collaborate about a variety of topics, such as helpful computer apps for students and teachers, curricula, and a variety of other school-related issues, such as grading systems. However, the real benefit for students and teachers is to maintain the focus on the four critical questions of a PLC. Many teams mistakenly believe their time should be spent on lesson planning, but lesson planning and curricula are not a part of the PLC process. In our work in schools, when we observe a team to find out its effectiveness, we look to connect the discussions members are having to one of the four PLC critical questions. If team members are not discussing aspects of their work that serve to answer at least one of those questions, their effectiveness will be limited.

The PLC Critical Questions on a Course-Alike Team

With the steps of finding a willing collaborative partner and committing to the team complete, the course-alike team can move on to answering the four critical questions of a PLC to do what PLC architect Robert Eaker (2020) notes is "the overarching work of teams . . . [it] must focus on enhancing the learning levels of all students, skill by skill" (p. 186). The following sections address this approach for each critical question.

Critical Question One

The work of teams in a PLC begins with answering the first critical question, "What knowledge, skills, and dispositions should every student acquire as a result of this unit, this course, or this grade level?" (DuFour et al., 2016, p. 36). To answer this question, a virtual team must prioritize the standards and decide which standards are essential, which are nice to know, and which the team is willing to sacrifice. Using REAL criteria (see chapter 3, page 33), the team must decide what all students must learn (Many & Horrell, 2014). The team members should also prepare to ask one another the guiding questions in figure 4.2 (page 54) so they don't end up answering questions two, three, and four for nonessential knowledge, skills, or dispositions.

After a virtual team gets clarity on the essential learning, members focus on setting SMART goals (DuFour et al., 2016). The team will need to determine the timeline for the unit and when to give the common formative assessment, and set a SMART goal for the essential learning. Figure 4.3 (page 55) guides teams in this process.

Determine Essential Learning—Discussion Guide

Unit: _____

Date: _____

Before the Unit Begins

Instructions: Complete this form prior to starting the unit to identify essential learning. This process involves unpacking standards into essential learning targets. Each essential learning target should go through this team process.

Guiding questions for educators to consider (REAL criteria):

1. **Does the learning develop student readiness for the next level of learning?** Is it essential for success in the next unit, course, or grade level?

2. **Does the essential have endurance?** Do teachers expect students to retain the knowledge and skills over time as opposed to merely learning them for a test?

3. **Do teachers assess the essential?** Will the essential learning be on state tests or college entrance, military, or trade school tests?

4. **Does the essential have leverage?** Will proficiency in the standard help students in other areas of the curriculum and other academic disciplines?

Resources to assist in making decisions:

- National, state or provincial, or local standards
- Unified district curricula
- Former lesson plans (what teachers taught versus what they intended to teach)
- State test samples
- Unit books
- Item analysis
- Prerequisite skills for the next course or grade level essential for success at that level

Essential learning for students to know and be able to do in this unit (no more than ten essentials per half year):

Nice-to-know learning (good material for extensions):

Willing to sacrifice:

Source: REAL criteria adapted from Many & Horrell, 2014. Copyright © 2021 by Brig Leane. Used with permission.

FIGURE 4.2: Course-alike team process for determining essential learning.

*Visit **go.SolutionTree.com/PLCbooks** to download a reproducible version of this figure.*

Create a SMART Goal—Discussion Guide

Unit: _____

Date: _____

<table>
<tr>
<td rowspan="8">Before the Unit Begins</td>
<td>Timeline</td>
<td>When does the unit begin and end?</td>
</tr>
<tr>
<td>Give common formative assessment on what date?</td>
<td>(Prior to the unit end date, so time is still available for interventions and extensions)</td>
</tr>
<tr>
<td>Team SMART goal for the unit of study

(The actual SMART goal is for team use only. Teachers should tell students they must all master the essential learning.)</td>
<td>Strategic and specific: Focuses on specific student learning; answers the questions, Who? and What?

Measurable: Teachers can measure the success toward meeting the goals in student achievement. It answers the question, How?

Attainable: Students can achieve the goal in a specific amount of time with increased teacher effectiveness. It should be a stretch from current achievement data.

Results oriented: The goal aligns with a school goal and focuses on increased student achievement in one defined area.

Time bound: The goal has a clear timeframe, including a target date. It answers the question, When?

Example: Seventy-five percent of sixth graders will be able to write arguments to support claims with clear reasons and relevant evidence by November 15.</td>
</tr>
<tr>
<td rowspan="3">Defining and communicating successes

How will we know when students have learned it?</td>
<td>What score equals proficiency? Is there a rubric? If so, attach it.

How will students know the essential learning?</td>
</tr>
<tr>
<td>How will teachers score the assessments to ensure inter-rater reliability?</td>
</tr>
<tr>
<td>When will teachers, students, and parents know who has and who has not learned the essential skill?</td>
</tr>
</table>

FIGURE 4.3: Course-alike team process for creating SMART goals.

*Visit **go.SolutionTree.com/PLCbooks** to download a reproducible version of this figure.*

Teams should consider how members will define and communicate success on the essential learning with one another, their students, and parents. Since members of virtual teams are from different schools or districts, they will likely have different expectations. Singletons should explore these differences (and similarities) to determine how they can best be collaborative partners.

Per figure 4.3, part of the collaborative process for singletons includes how to make the essential learning clear to students—a great professional discussion among virtual team members that will significantly impact students' ability to hit the learning targets. Like a basketball hoop in a gym, students should clearly see the target for the unit. Teachers can use visuals like a thermometer on a bulletin board labeled with the essential skill and percent proficient in the class to communicate progress toward the goal. Next to the thermometer could be exemplars of what proficient work looks like or a rubric detailing expectations. There could also be a word wall with the vocabulary the unit uses that students will need to know to become proficient.

Parents should also be made aware of the essentials prior to the unit and how they can help support their child. This could include video links parents watch with their child, printouts of practice work specifically addressing the essential learning they can work on together, or questions parents could ask to help them gauge their child's level of understanding related to the essential learning. In addition, students and parents should receive feedback on whether a student has demonstrated proficiency and what the student's next steps are based on that feedback. This could be done with a group email (using blind cc, of course) to the group of parents whose child hasn't yet demonstrated proficiency, along with a description of how the parents could help support their child and how the school team is supporting the student as well. An email to those who have demonstrated proficiency is always appreciated. This should be done in a separate email from each campus.

Teacher teams should be monitoring team SMART goals to see how close all the students are to proficiency of the essential. Keep this information in an electronic team binder or on a shared drive. Since privacy of student records is a legal limitation, teams should consider using their shared drives for team materials, but keep their own records of which students have and haven't yet mastered the essential learning.

Critical Question Two

The work of a course-alike virtual team continues with answering the second critical question, "How will we know when each student has acquired the essential knowledge and skills?" (DuFour et al., 2016, p. 36). Teachers can accomplish this by having students attempt a team-created common formative assessment. While we don't have a template for a specific assessment design since subjects vary so greatly, the idea is to keep the focus of the assessment on the essential learning. The assessment can be very rigorous, but it does not need to be lengthy. It could take the form of an exit ticket, a quiz, a project, an oral response—any one of a variety of ways to assess if learning took place. However, if the assessment is measuring multiple standards or learning targets, developing an intervention response becomes more difficult because of the need to address a broader range of individual student learning needs. In our experiences, teachers are more likely to intervene when there are fewer standards or targets to respond to.

Teammates should give common formative assessments on the same day, if possible, and administer them with similar directions and similar assistance. This matters for a virtual team because members who have more time to teach the essential learning should expect their students to perform at higher levels. When teachers have the same amount of time to teach, the main variable in student success becomes the best instructional strategies—the very thing that teams working through the PLC process are trying to determine. If a team begins to administer assessments on different days, this delays the response plan for students who haven't learned.

After giving a common formative assessment, virtual teams must ensure they are grading the assessments the same way, as inter-rater reliability is a prerequisite to sharing team data in a meaningful way. Having the team look at ungraded student work without discussion until each teacher determines a final grade on the assessment usually accomplishes inter-rater reliability. Share the grade and the rationale for the grade each teacher gives among the group. This process is repeated with several assessments to ensure the way one member grades an assessment matches the way another member grades the same assessment. A tremendous amount of professional growth occurs during the inter-rater reliability process, and if skipped, tends to invalidate the next step: the sharing of results to determine best practices. Virtual teams could take screenshots of ungraded student work, share screens during a Zoom call, and then see if members are grading the same piece of student work the same way. If virtual teams are using a rubric, members can independently score student work using the rubric and check with one another to see if each member is consistently applying the rubric. If the team is using selected-response questions, the team members need to ensure they are using the same criteria for success (for example, two of three correct equals proficiency). Creating inter-rater reliability ensures true comparable data, which teams need to determine effective practices.

After establishing inter-rater reliability, teachers grade the rest of their students' common formative assessments and get ready to share the percent of their students who are proficient at the next meeting. This sharing is not intended to judge one another but to find out which teaching techniques were the most effective in the challenging task of getting students to learn the essential.

Critical Questions Three and Four

When teams are ready to share their results, and they know student by student who has and has not learned the essential, they are ready to complete the action plan for critical questions three and four ("How will we respond when some students do not learn?" and "How will we extend the learning for students who are already proficient?"; DuFour et al., 2016, p. 36). The template in figure 4.4 guides teams through the discussions that effective teams should be having as they work through critical questions three and four.

Once teachers carry out the action plan in figure 4.4, it is important for the team to see how it did in meeting its SMART goal and capture any additional team learning that occurred after the interventions. If the teachers learned new skills through the interventions, they should consider using those skills during the initial instruction the next time they teach the essential learning. The template in figure 4.5 (page 60) will guide virtual teams through the remainder of the collaborative team process to determine how well the team did at meeting the goal, capture any effective intervention strategies, and record any additional team learning.

For teams with more experience in the PLC process, products might look much shorter and have fewer details than those in this chapter. For these teams, we recommend members still determine the essential learning, a SMART goal for the essential learning, and the current overall percentage of student proficiency, and record team learning. Teams could easily capture this information on one page to submit for leadership team review. An example of a shortened template is in chapter 7 (page 105). The members then share feedback they receive about team products with the rest of the virtual team. Teams should share only percentages of students who are proficient—not student names—across different schools. Often when starting out, the additional guidance of the templates in this chapter is helpful.

Action Plan for Intervention and Extension—Discussion Guide

Unit: _____

Date: _____

Instructions: Complete this section when the collaborative team has given the common formative assessment, graded it, and is ready to discuss the results.

After the Common Formative Assessment		
Which students need more time and support on this essential skill? (Each teacher should keep his or her own list of students.)	
How will the teacher provide that time and support?	
What is the extension plan for those who are already proficient?	
Timeline What is the time period for these interventions? When will the teacher reassess the students to see if they are proficient after the intervention?	
Based on the data from shared results, what are the most effective strategies from teachers' initial instruction? What changes to instruction should the team make?	
If there were areas where all teachers' students struggled, what is the team plan to get outside assistance? (For example, is there an instructional coach with expertise? Has the grade or course above or below the students' current level identified a successful strategy?)	

FIGURE 4.4: Action plan for intervention and extension.

*Visit **go.SolutionTree.com/PLCbooks** to download a reproducible version of this figure.*

			Unit: _____
Final Data and Reflection on Changes to Instruction—Discussion Guide			Date: _____

Instructions: Complete this section after a team has carried out the Action Plan for Intervention and Extension.

<table>
<tr><td rowspan="4" style="vertical-align:middle">After the Team Implements the Action Plan</td><td rowspan="2">What was the team SMART goal identified at the beginning of the unit?</td><td rowspan="2"></td><td>After all interventions, what percent of students was proficient in this essential learning?</td><td></td></tr>
<tr><td>Did the team meet the goal?</td><td></td></tr>
<tr><td>What intervention strategies were the most effective for students who did not learn the essential the first time?

What additional changes to instruction should the team make?</td><td colspan="3">This is also a time to capture changes the team should make to the essential learning, assessment, intervention plans, or initial instructional techniques.</td></tr>
<tr><td>What is the team plan for those students who still don't demonstrate proficiency in the essential skill, even after the interventions?</td><td colspan="3"></td></tr>
</table>

FIGURE 4.5: Final data and reflection on changes to instruction for course-alike teams.

*Visit **go.SolutionTree.com/PLCbooks** to download a reproducible version of this figure.*

Perspectives From the Field

When I first began teaching, I was concerned that my life experiences didn't really align with the subject I signed up for. I felt as though I was not fully prepared to teach technology and engineering, but I was willing to try. Fortunately, the teacher I was replacing suggested I join this collaborative group of other technology-ed teachers in the same district. Joining the team was incredibly beneficial to me and my program.

We have met once a month and during every in-service for all the years I have been a teacher. In the beginning, the district offered an incentive to meet as a team after hours. The team felt the incentive was nice, but members knew collaboration was the real value. When that incentive went away, the team chose to continue to meet on the members' own time; we felt the collaboration was that valuable to our practice.

During our time together, we have created and analyzed formative and summative assessments, essential skills, and standards-based projects. These collaborative products have made a huge impact on our teaching and our students.

For instance, after one particular session when a seasoned teacher admitted he was struggling with his students' engagement in class, we suggested he try moving to a modular format with more student choices. He tried it the very next day and reported that it transformed his classroom and his students on the spot. Another seasoned teacher also tried the model and said the transformation in his students and his class made him a better teacher.

New teachers coming to our team have also been incredibly thankful for the team-created products, and our willingness to collaborate and share. After all, we all want the same thing—to have a great program where students have the opportunity to create and learn.

My advice to teachers who are singletons in their buildings is to invest in collaborating with other similar teachers, let your guard down, be willing to try something new, and be willing to give your experience and knowledge to others. If there are not enough teachers in your district, find some in other districts. Based on my experience, you and your students will be glad you did.

—Darrell K., singleton tech-ed teacher

A Note for Leaders: Providing Support

When possible, all teachers who teach the same course or grade level should be on the same team, with the same planning time, and with classrooms as close to one another as possible for collaboration, as well as for sharing students. But most of these supports will not work for singletons who collaborate electronically, and yet leaders still need to know how singleton collaboration is progressing.

As a leader, it is critical to know which teams need more time and support to be able to work through the PLC process. Leaders can only delegate the PLC process to those teams with both the skill (knowledge of how to go through the PLC process) and the will (willingness to consistently work through the PLC process) to do the work. Leaders should observe those teams periodically to see if members are following their norms and to be available for assistance or questions. Being present sends the message this is important work. Teams that lack the skill or the will also need your presence. Do not hand a template to singletons with the message, "Turn this in;" instead, work together with teams on the template while members try the first few times. There will be struggles, and teams will need help and encouragement. Your presence with the teams—even via Zoom—will help answer questions and let teams know you value the work.

In addition, provide singleton teachers with flexibility for virtual meetings. For instance, if two teachers from two different campuses who teach middle school band want to collaborate but don't have common planning time, they could agree to a Google Meet or Zoom once per week for an hour after school. Excuse those teachers from weekly in-school collaboration time, as long as they were able to generate the critical work products that teams should be producing.

Given that teams collaborating virtually are constructed across school, district, and perhaps state lines, leaders should connect with the leaders of those other schools to discuss collaboration expectations and how best to support the virtual team. This discussion could reduce overlapping efforts and should address contradictory team expectations on different campuses. In addition, communication between school leaders is important any time a virtual team is struggling to work through the four critical questions of a PLC.

Why Do It? Course-Alike Teams

In our work in schools, we hear many reasons—or, more accurately, excuses—singleton teachers and leaders may have for not wanting to do the work of collaboration. Do any of these reasons resonate with you?

- **Reasons to Not Do the Work**
  - "The other teachers in the district who teach my subject aren't interested in working together, and we wouldn't get along anyway."
  - "It can be embarrassing to share results with people I don't know that well."
  - "There is not enough time to do the work we already have on our plates. Why add more?"
  - "It can be hard to find another same-course colleague at another campus."

▸ "It's probably not possible to find time to collaborate or to align schedules with teachers from other campuses."

▸ "Expectations for each teacher on different campuses can vary significantly."

It is true that moving from working as an isolated singleton to being a member of a course-alike virtual team will result in a loss of some autonomy; however, staying in isolation is a recipe for mediocrity.

- **Reasons to Do the Work**

  ▸ Teams create synergy and save time. There are many examples of similar work singleton teachers need to do on any campus, such as determining the essential learning in a unit, creating assessments to measure student learning, developing action plans, and reflecting on the unit. There's no reason for each individual to duplicate these tasks when electronic collaboration is so readily available.

  ▸ Teams provide support for new teachers. New teachers can quickly become overloaded with tasks, and combined with insufficient support and resources, they can lose hope. But when teamed with another teacher of the same subject who agrees to a common essential focus, with a willingness to share the workload and a commitment to learning together through the process, new teachers receive much needed support and affirmation.

  ▸ Teams provide opportunities to learn from experienced teachers. When an experienced teacher retires, all of his or her knowledge walks right out the door, unless the retiring teacher had the time and structures in place to share his or her knowledge with a colleague in another building in a way that didn't seem opinionated, but instead was based on results.

  ▸ No teacher should be isolated, as isolation is the enemy of improvement. Effective methods exist to easily connect singletons with other singletons.

Conclusion

This on-ramp to collaboration is often the most meaningful, as the day-to-day content of the colleagues is usually so similar. Before the COVID-19 pandemic, connecting over a computer might have felt like some futuristic way to communicate only for the tech savvy. Now, however, making a Zoom call and working remotely aren't such a big deal, and the virtual team can take advantage of this technology. But for those singletons who are not ready to collaborate across schools, or those who have not found that virtual team yet, they might find their best collaborative option to be the common-content on-ramp we discuss in the next chapter.

Tools and Resources

Refer to these tools and resources to learn more about the content covered in this chapter.

Educators who are looking for additional perspectives related to virtual teams should see the following resources.

- *Learning by Doing* (DuFour et al., 2016, pp. 61–62, Electronic Teams)

- *How to Develop PLCs for Singletons and Small Schools* (Hansen, 2015, pp. 45–56, Virtual Teams)

CHAPTER 5

Common-Content On-Ramp

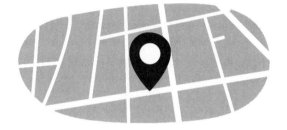

The most valuable resource that all teachers have is each other. Without collaboration, our growth is limited to our own perspectives.

—Robert John Meehan

Malik was stumped. The administrators at Sequoia Elementary had asked him to begin collaborating with the other social studies teacher at his school, Jackie, but they didn't teach any of the same courses. In the other core subjects at his school, every teacher taught the same course as at least one other teacher, and was excited to have weekly time set aside to collaborate on this common course. Malik didn't know how to get started collaborating with Jackie. They couldn't write assessments together since they were writing them for different courses. They could share data on how students were doing in their classes, but Malik didn't see how that would help them. Malik wanted to do what his administrators asked, but frustration was already setting in. He wanted to do the right thing, but he didn't know what that was and he wasn't getting much help.

Meanwhile, at the district's other elementary school, Jamie, the principal, was thinking it was a no-brainer for the two third-grade teachers in her school to be on the same collaborative team; the problem was, third grade was the only grade with two teachers. Jamie wondered what to do about the singleton fourth-grade and singleton fifth-grade teachers in her building. She thought perhaps she could combine the primary grades teachers into one team, and maybe the fourth- and fifth-grade teachers could be a team of two as well. But the struggle seemed to be that the curricula for these classes were so different. Jamie wondered if the collaboration would feel forced or if there could be any professional benefit to the teachers by having them collaborate.

Pause and Reflect

TEACHERS

- Even though singletons do not have common courses, in what ways could they identify common knowledge or skills to collaborate about?
- Could singletons come to consensus on what proficiency in common skills looks like?
- How might singletons collaborate about essential schoolwide academic behaviors?

LEADERS

- In what ways could teachers of different grade levels find meaningful collaboration?
- Are there any skills that cut across grade levels or subjects, even when the content isn't the same?

As a singleton, it is very easy to feel isolated knowing you are the only person teaching a specific course or grade level. This sense of isolation can be exacerbated if you are in a school where the large majority of staff is on collaborative teams with someone else who teaches the exact same course or grade level. As we work with singletons from a wide range of content areas and grade levels, and we closely examine the content they teach, we discover they have more content in common than they may have previously thought. This chapter explores the common-content on-ramp. It discusses what common content is, how to maximize common pacing, tackling the PLC critical questions, and guiding decision making. It ends with a note for leaders and reasons to do the work.

What Is Common Content?

So, what do we mean by *common content*? The content any teacher in a PLC teaches originates with an examination of the first of the four PLC critical questions: "What knowledge, skills, and dispositions should every student acquire as a result of this unit, this course, or this grade level?" (DuFour et al., 2016, p. 36). As stated in chapter 3 (page 29), the collaborative process begins with teachers each identifying the essential learning for every course they teach. These essentials specifically identify the knowledge, skills, and dispositions every student is to acquire in the unit, course, or grade level. Based on national, state or provincial, or local standards, these identified essentials become the guaranteed and viable curriculum (Marzano, 2018). *Common content* is simply the knowledge, skills, or dispositions that two or more teachers each identify as essential.

When we begin working with singletons, we often hear comments such as, "We don't have anything in common. We don't teach the same class." Most often, these comments come from singletons who have never placed their essential learning documents side by side with another singleton's documents and looked at the specific skills both of them teach. Let's examine three different examples of specific common content singleton teachers identify as essential in mathematics, history, and science.

- **Mathematics example:** The following three teachers each teach place value understanding. However, the application of place value in the skill of rounding increases in complexity over three years.

  ▸ *Third-grade mathematics teacher*—Use place value understanding to round whole numbers to the nearest 10 or 100 (3.NBT.1; California Department of Education, 2013b).

  ▸ *Fourth-grade mathematics teacher*—Use place value understanding to round multidigit whole numbers to any place (4.NBT.3; California Department of Education, 2013b).

  ▸ *Fifth-grade mathematics teacher*—Use place value understanding to round decimals to any place (5.NBT.4; California Department of Education, 2013b).

- **History example:** These teachers, teaching two entirely different courses, both identify the skill of citing textual evidence as essential. The skill is the same, but increases in complexity from one course to the next.

> ▸ *World history teacher*—Cite specific textual evidence to support
> analysis of primary and secondary sources, attending to such features
> as the date and origin of the information (RH.9–10.1; California
> Department of Education, 2013a).

> > ▸ *U.S. history teacher*—Cite specific textual evidence to support analysis
> > of primary and secondary sources, connecting insights gained from
> > specific details to an understanding of the text as a whole (RH.11–
> > 12.1; California Department of Education, 2013a).

- **Science example:** Even though one teacher is teaching about the
cycling of matter and energy, and the other is teaching about matter
and chemical reactions, they both have to develop their students' skill of
using mathematical representations to support a claim.

  > ▸ *Biology teacher*—Use mathematical representations to support claims
  > for the cycling of matter and flow of energy among organisms in an
  > ecosystem (BI-LS2–4; Arkansas Department of Education, 2016a).

  > ▸ *Chemistry teacher*—Use mathematical representations to support the
  > claim that atoms, and therefore mass, are conserved during a chemical
  > reaction (CI-PS1–7, Arkansas Department of Education, 2016b).

As you see in the three preceding examples, the essentials are not identical, but the
skills are common. Rounding a number, citing textual evidence, and using mathematical representations are skills each of these singleton examples have in common.
Finding common content provides the foundation for meaningful collaboration in
singleton teams.

Maximize Common Pacing

Once teachers, or a collaborative team of teachers, identify the essential learning, they then turn to creating a pacing guide for the year or course. The purpose
of the pacing guide is to determine the sequence to teach the essentials and how
much time to devote to them throughout the school year to ensure there is adequate
time to effectively teach, assess, and provide interventions when needed. Most teams
and teachers create units of instruction that include all their identified essentials. In
Taking Action, RTI experts and coauthors Austin Buffum, Mike Mattos, and Janet
Malone (2018) outline the following four steps for creating essential unit plans:

1. Analyze and discuss the type of learning each essential standard requires
   of students (knowledge, reasoning, performance skills, and products; par-
   enthetical added)

2. Deconstruct each essential standard to identify learning targets

3. Convert learning targets into student-friendly language

4. Collaboratively create or select assessments to administer throughout the unit of study and agree on when to administer them (p. 90)

The most powerful way to utilize the common content singletons identify is to teach and assess the common content within the same timeframe of the same unit. This allows the singletons to engage in the following powerful collaborative work.

1. Plan instruction and develop lessons on common content.

2. Create a common assessment or common rubric.

3. Reflect and discuss their instructional effectiveness throughout and at the conclusion of the unit.

4. Compare their results utilizing the common assessment or common rubric and collaboratively develop intervention plans.

Creating common pacing between two teachers teaching the same course is relatively simple. However, singleton teachers who do not teach the same course will have some content in common and some content not in common. This non-common content makes it much more complex to teach what the teachers do have in common at the same time. When singletons determine the sequence of the essential learning, they must carefully consider the connections between the essentials. History teachers will logically sequence their essential learning chronologically. Mathematics teachers will look at how one essential learning is foundational or a prerequisite to developing proficiency on another essential and sequence accordingly. Teachers each utilize their knowledge of the essential learning and carefully sequence it to maximize student learning.

Knowing that teaching common content at the same time is a goal of collaboration, singletons on common-content teams should maximize the opportunities to align their pacing guides. We ask singleton teams to ponder this key question: "Can we organize our pacing guides to teach our identified common content at the same time without jeopardizing the appropriate sequence of any course or grade level?" For non-common content, we recommend using the critical-friend on-ramp process we explain in chapter 6 (page 87). But we recommend focusing on the common content initially. As a team's capacity increases, begin collaborating about the non-common content.

We find some essentials are easier to teach at the same time than others. The two history teachers from the previous example typically find it relatively easy to teach citing textual evidence at the same time because they can teach that skill with any history content. However, the biology and chemistry teachers might struggle to teach using mathematical representations at the same time if teaching units on cycling of matter and energy (biology) and teaching matter and chemical reactions (chemistry) do not occur at the same time in their respective courses. Our experience shows that by closely examining each course's pacing guide and looking to align common content, every singleton team will be able to teach some of its common content at the same time. For common content for which teams can't align the pacing, we once again recommend utilizing the critical-friend on-ramp (see chapter 6, page 87).

The PLC Critical Questions on a Common-Content Team

With the steps of finding a willing collaborative partner and committing to the team complete, the common-content team can move on to answering the four critical questions of a PLC.

Critical Question One

The common-content on-ramp into meaningful collaboration requires a team of singletons to identify content they have in common and create common pacing. To identify common content, all team members must identify their course's essential learning (see chapter 3, page 29).

COMMON CONTENT

As part of the unpacking process, each team member uses the essential learning to identify the skills he or she teaches by looking at the verbs in the standards. Consider the earlier example of the history teachers.

- **World history teacher:** Cite specific textual evidence to support analysis of primary and secondary sources, attending to such features as the date and origin of the information (RH.9–10.1; California Department of Education, 2013a).

- **U.S. history teacher:** Cite specific textual evidence to support analysis of primary and secondary sources, connecting insights gained from specific details to an understanding of the text as a whole (RH.11–12.1; California Department of Education, 2013a).

The verb in both their standards is *cite*. Both teachers must teach their students to cite. Next, circle all the verbs (skills) in the essentials. As they begin to circle all the verbs (skills), most singletons will begin discovering many skills they teach in common.

After circling and identifying the skills (verbs), teachers each should identify all the concepts, facts, and knowledge for their specific course or courses. They accomplish this by underlining all the nouns and noun phrases following the verbs. Using the previous world history and U.S. history example, singleton team members would underline the phrase, *specific textual evidence to support analysis of primary and secondary sources.*

Knowing the skill is to cite, the teachers also know students must cite specific textual evidence to support analysis of primary and secondary sources. For this example, not only do the singletons teach the same skill but they also teach the same concept of citing to support the analysis.

Singletons often find they teach the same skill as their team members, such as analyze, but the concepts or knowledge are different. Let's examine two other essentials for the same two history teachers from the previous example.

- **World history teacher:** Students analyze the effect of the Industrial Revolution. (WH.10.3; California Department of Education, 2000)

- **U.S. history teacher:** Students analyze America's participation in World War II. (USH.11.7; California Department of Education, 2000)

Both the world history and U.S. history teachers must teach their students the exact same essential skill of analyzing, but the knowledge they have to analyze is quite different. One is teaching students to analyze the effect of the Industrial Revolution, while the other is teaching students to analyze America's participation in World War II. This is expected and doesn't inhibit common-content teachers from collaborating about formative assessment.

As you examine the skills across subjects and grade levels, you will see many commonalities despite the presence of non-common content. Students must learn skills such as describing, analyzing, identifying, and comparing and contrasting in most content areas and at almost all grade levels. It is the concepts or knowledge of the course that varies. These common skills provide a great foundation for meaningful collaboration for singletons.

There is another source of common content that common-content singleton teams should examine: behaviors. Schools often identify dispositions that include academic behaviors or social behaviors as part of schoolwide essential learning. For example, maybe your school administrators state they want all students to proficiently collaborate with others as an essential social behavior. Such schoolwide essential learnings are another important source of common content for singleton teams.

For example, a FACS (family and consumer science) teacher and an EAST (education accelerated by service and technology) teacher decide even though they don't share a common curriculum, they do share several dispositions they both deem essential as outcomes for their students. Here is their list of essentials they decided to collaborate about.

1. Ability to self-assess

2. Ability to collaborate effectively with others

3. Ability to keep projects and workspace organized

4. Ability to problem solve and have grit when challenges arise

COMMON PACING

Now that a team has identified common content, the next key step is to maximize common pacing. As stated earlier, singletons on common-content teams will be able to teach some common content at the same time, but not all. We have yet to find a singleton team that can teach all the common content at the same time. Teachers will be using the critical-friend on-ramp (see chapter 6, page 87) for all non-common content, so they do not need to create common pacing for that portion of their content.

Once they identify the common content, team members review their pacing guides to see where the skills fall during the curriculum timeline. Team members should first look for those skills they already teach at the same time and highlight them. Now look to see if there are any common skills taught close to the same time period. With some minor adjustments, these skills could be taught at the same time. Congratulations, you've just discovered what you can collaborate about!

Next, identify any common skills, concepts, facts, or knowledge with flexibility about when you can teach it. When could you and other team members teach it using the same start and end dates that fit within your pacing guide? When making these critical pacing decisions, use the same guiding question we previously introduced, "Can we organize our pacing guides to teach our identified common content at the same time without jeopardizing the appropriate sequence of any course or grade level?" For example, the world history and U.S. history teachers could decide to teach citing textual evidence beginning the sixth week of school.

Finally, work with team members to set common pacing for the identified common content. If a school has established key organizational academic skills, the team could decide to teach them during the first few weeks of school to set the stage for a successful year. Figure 5.1 is a template singletons on common-content teams can use to identify the common content among the different team members.

Critical Question One—Discussion Guide

Unit: _____

Date: _____

Instructions: With your collaborative team members, follow these steps to identify the content (knowledge, skills, dispositions) you have in common.

Determining Common Content

1. Circle and closely examine the verbs of your essential learning to identify the skills you teach in your course. Do you teach any of the same skills as a team member? List these common skills.

2. Underline and closely examine the nouns or noun phrases of your essentials to identify the concepts, facts, or knowledge in your course. Do you have anything in common with a team member? List these common concepts, facts, and knowledge.

3. Has your school or department identified essential student dispositions you teach? Do you have any dispositions in common with a team member? List these dispositions.

Maximizing Common Pacing

1. Place your established pacing guides next to each other. Highlight any of the skills, concepts, facts, or knowledge identified in the previous steps that you teach at a similar time. Could you adjust your pacing guides slightly without jeopardizing the sequence of your content to allow you to teach them at the same time? If so, adjust your pacing guides accordingly.

2. Highlight any of the skills, concepts, facts, or knowledge identified in the previous steps that you have flexibility with when you teach it. Discuss and come to consensus when you will teach these, including start and end dates.

3. For the identified common student dispositions, discuss and come to consensus when you will teach these, including start and end dates.

FIGURE 5.1: Common-content template for PLC critical question one.
*Visit **go.SolutionTree.com/PLCbooks** to download a reproducible version of this figure.*

Critical Question Two

Creating and utilizing common formative assessments with singletons are an often misunderstood process; therefore, common formative assessments often are either nonexistent or underutilized in singleton teams. The key to creating common formative assessments as a singleton team is to focus on what members have in common. Going back to the two history teachers, both teachers are teaching students to cite textual evidence to support analysis of primary and secondary sources. The next step for teams is to clearly define what proficiency looks like for this skill. We recommend the use of common rubrics, which allow team members to clearly define the different levels of proficiency and apply a common tool. See figure 5.2 (page 74) for an example of what such a rubric might look like.

	Beginning	Developing	Proficient	Beyond Proficient
Text evidence	Does not reference text evidence	Cites evidence from the text by using either direct quotes or paraphrasing	Cites evidence from the text by using both direct quotes and paraphrasing	Skillfully blends evidence from the text by using both direct quotes and paraphrasing
Explanation of evidence	Provides no or incorrect explanation or analysis of how text details support the question asked	Provides some explanation or analysis of how text details support the question asked	Provides clear explanation or analysis of how text details support the question asked	Provides insightful explanation or analysis of how text details support the question asked
Quantity and quality of evidence	Provides very little or unrelated or incorrect evidence to support opinion	Provides limited or vague evidence to support opinion	Provides enough related evidence to support opinion	Provides more than enough and the strongest evidence to support opinion

FIGURE 5.2: Sample common rubric for common-content singleton team.

In *Simplifying Common Assessment,* assessment and PLC process consultants Kim Bailey and Chris Jakicic (2017) "recommend vertical teams consider two ways of thinking about what they have in common: (1) specific skills that are the same and taught in each of their content areas or grades and (2) skills that developed through a learning progression" (pp. 108–109). Therefore, a team might consider developing a rubric that grows in complexity from one grade level to the next. Teams may start with a common rubric for a specific skill, as figure 5.2 illustrates, but will evolve it into a rubric that shows the progression of the standard through each grade level. Figure 5.3 shows how the complexity of identifying the main idea increases from grades 3–5.

Learning Target	Third-Grade Proficiency	Fourth-Grade Proficiency	Fifth-Grade Proficiency
Identify and support the main idea of a text.	Determine the main idea by identifying key details that support it.	Determine the main idea and explain how key details support it.	Determine two or more main ideas and explain how key details support each main idea.

FIGURE 5.3: Rubric with standard progression.

With a common rubric in place, the singleton team can apply it together in its specific content area. Using the world history and U.S. history examples again, teachers each select the primary and secondary sources for their content and assess students using the common rubric. As with any rubric, it will be important to create inter-rater reliability by scoring the writing together to ensure all team members are consistently applying it. Even though the source documents are different, the skill of citing is common when you use a common rubric and ensure inter-rater reliability.

For those instances when you are not teaching the common content at the same time due to pacing issues, team members each can still use the rubric when they are teaching the skill. This promotes consistency and common understanding for both teachers and students. You can still create inter-rater reliability, but the work samples will only come from one teacher.

Finally, teams often find it helpful to begin collecting student samples that best demonstrate the different levels of proficiency for the different characteristics in the rubric. Teachers can use these samples to build shared and consistent understanding of the rubric. Share student samples with new team members as they learn the curriculum. Just as important, if not more important, is to share samples with students to build their clarity of what proficiency looks like. Figure 5.4 is a template to develop a common formative assessment for your identified common content.

Critical Question Two—Discussion Guide   Unit: _____

Date: _____

Instructions: With your collaborative team members, follow these steps to create and utilize a common rubric for a team-developed common formative assessment.

Developing the Rubric

1. Determine the common skill for which to build a rubric.

2. Examine your standards documents to build knowledge of the standard.

3. Examine any existing state, regional or provincial, or local rubrics for the identified skill, including those from other content areas.

4. Identify what you want to assess. This will form the criteria for the skill and assessment.

5. Identify the characteristics you will assess. These will become the far left-hand column on the rubric. Be careful to limit the characteristics to just those you determine most important.

FIGURE 5.4: Common-content template for PLC critical question two.   continued →

6. Describe the level of mastery for each characteristic. These will be the cells in each row. Often these contain clear language about the quality and quantity of what you expect.

Creating Inter-rater Reliability

1. Collect multiple samples (approximately four or five) of student work in which to apply the rubric. Make multiple copies of each work sample.

2. Read the rubric together and ask and answer any questions to develop increased common understanding.

3. Individually score a selected piece of work.

4. Share your scores for each characteristic. Discuss any disparities in scoring, and come to agreement.

5. Repeat steps 3–4 with additional work samples until there is little or no disparity in applying the rubric.

Visit **go.SolutionTree.com/PLCbooks** to download a reproducible version of this figure.

Critical Questions Three and Four

With common content identified and common formative assessments (common rubrics) in place, the exciting work of utilizing the data comes next. The word we want to focus on is *formative*. In *Embedded Formative Assessment*, Dylan Wiliam (2011), professor emeritus of educational assessment at University College London's (UCL's) Institute of Education, defines *formative assessment* as "encompassing all those activities taken by teachers, and/or by their students, which provide information to be used as feedback to modify the teaching and learning activities in which they were engaged" (p. 37). As all assessment experts state, an assessment is only formative when you use it formatively.

There are three major purposes of formative assessments.

1. Monitoring and responding to individual student progress

2. Analyzing and impacting individual and team instructional effectiveness

3. Students reflecting on their learning

MONITORING AND RESPONDING TO INDIVIDUAL STUDENT PROGRESS

Using common rubrics, team members can identify the specific skills or portions of skills students need more support with. Once that's done, singleton team members develop an action plan, which may also be thought of as a response plan. An *action plan* consists of the following elements (Dimich, 2015).

1. Identify the misconception, error, or difficulty needing support.

2. List of students needing the support

3. Instructional plan to provide the support

4. Reassessment plan to determine proficiency level after providing additional time and support

Teachers should implement the response plan individually or collectively as a collaborative team. In most cases, a singleton team will respond to its students individually because members are not teaching the common content at the same time, the knowledge aspect of the common skill is different, or they do not have access to their students at the same time. Of course, members of a virtual team will respond individually. To best meet the needs of the students of team members on the same campus, we encourage team members to have students receive intervention from any teacher on the team when the following is true.

1. Team members teach the common content at the same time.

2. Team members have access to their students at the same time.

3. It is beneficial for team members to share students to meet students' specific needs.

ANALYZING AND IMPACTING INDIVIDUAL AND TEAM INSTRUCTIONAL EFFECTIVENESS

The patterns, successes, and failures in formative assessment results give you insights into your individual and collective instructional effectiveness. With the focus on learning, teams can begin to see which aspects of instruction are most successful and which aspects are less effective. When teams do this analysis collectively as a team of teachers using a common formative assessment and having comparative data, they open the opportunity to learn how someone else on the team may have a more effective instructional strategy. Asking one another, "Did anyone have success with [fill in the blank]? I see your students performed better here; tell me what you did," examining comparable data together, and collectively seeking more effective strategies are the highest-leverage collaborative team actions any team can participate in. Team members can use this new learning and identification of more effective instructional practices immediately when providing interventions to the students still needing support and, in the future, when teaching the same or similar skill.

STUDENTS REFLECTING ON THEIR LEARNING

The final major purpose of the formative assessment is to involve the students. Students often think school and grades are happening *to* them. Using formative assessments allows students to reflect on their learning, so they can better understand their current level of learning and how to better continue their learning. Coauthors Connie M. Moss and Susan M. Brookhart (2019) state that "if students are not gathering and using evidence from their own work to improve learning, then what is happening does not meet our definition of formative assessment" (p. 3).

A common and successful approach to student reflection is providing students with a rubric and exemplary student samples, then asking students to compare these with their work. Students can do this individually or cooperatively with other students. Student self-reflection questions could include the following.

- "What would I have to change in my work to move from developing to proficient?"

- "What did my classmate do that I didn't do that would improve my work?"

Encouraging and providing opportunities for students to revise and demonstrate their learning at a higher level promote ownership and engagement. Through this personal reflection, students begin to see the purpose of intervention and know more specifically what they need to improve. Coauthors and educational consultants Tim Brown and William M. Ferriter (2021) explore this topic in great detail in their book *You Can Learn! Building Student Ownership, Motivation, and Efficacy With the PLC at Work Process*, providing multiple examples of what it may look like in the classroom, including having students reflect on practice tests before attempting a final demonstration of mastery, developing student action plans after formative assessments in a unit, or using extension menus for each unit.

Student self-reflection creates clear connections between the common formative assessment, common-content rubric, and next steps for improving. For students who already demonstrate proficiency or exceeded proficiency, self-reflection also provides students time to learn and demonstrate their learning at an even higher level. Use the template in figure 5.5 to plan and provide students with intervention and extension.

Critical Questions Three and Four—Discussion Guide

Unit: _____

Date: _____

Instructions: With your collaborative team members, follow these steps to utilize the evidence of student learning formatively.

Monitoring and Responding to Individual Student Learning

1. Referring to the common rubric, identify the misconceptions, errors, and difficulties for each student. If a student has more than one, determine what is most significant.

2. Make a list of students who need additional support, grouping students by common misconceptions, errors, and difficulty. Sometimes this involves grouping students with similar difficulties.

3. For each group of students and their corresponding difficulty, work with your team members to identify the most successful instructional strategies. (You will choose which ones to use in a later step.)

4. Determine how you will reassess your students after providing additional support. This may consist of students submitting new work for teachers to score against the rubric or revising students' current work to reassess it with the same rubric.

5. Determine when you will provide the additional support. This can be done during designated core instruction time or during designated intervention time when you have access to your students.

6. Implement the response plan and reassess students.

Analyzing and Impacting Instructional Effectiveness

1. Complete a data table that shows your proficiency rates for each characteristic of the rubric comparable between team members.

2. Examine and analyze the data, looking for positive differences.

3. Discuss the instructional strategies and practices that led to these positive differences. This may include a teacher sharing instructional resources or modeling strategies.

4. From the strategies you identify, choose the instructional strategies you will use when providing interventions.

5. Capture the key points about the most effective instructional strategies and note them in your unit plans to utilize in the future.

Students Reflecting on Their Learning

1. Provide students with the common rubric, exemplar student work, and their own work.

2. Individually, or in groups while examining the rubric and exemplars, ask students to identify what they need to improve to increase their level of proficiency.

3. Ask students to continue to reflect as they engage in intervention or reassessment, or revise their current work.

FIGURE 5.5: Common-content template for PLC critical questions three and four.

*Visit **go.SolutionTree.com/PLCbooks** to download a reproducible version of this figure.*

Pause and Reflect

- Has your team taken the time to identify the skills and concepts members all teach? Can members teach them at the same time?

- Which of the common skills the team identifies are the highest priority?

- What rubric should the team create about a common skill or concept to begin?

- What might be an easy first step to begin helping students reflect on their learning?

- How might you help your singleton teams discover what members teach in common?

- Do your singleton teams know how to build a rubric? If not, how can you build their capacity?

- What feedback do you need to give as singletons begin to identify their common content?

More Ideas for Collaboration

Sometimes singleton teachers will still struggle finding worthy essential learning about which to collaborate with another colleague, depending on their specific assignments. We discovered some literacy standards and skills that are essential across multiple disciplines teachers can use to ensure meaningful collaboration. While this list is not exhaustive, it will help any singleton team generate additional ideas for meaningful collaboration. Following are possible ideas of essential learning for singletons to consider as common content.

Specific standards (National Governors Association Center for Best Practices [NGA] & Council of Chief State School Officers [CCSSO], 2010):

- Come to discussions prepared, having read or studied required material; explicitly draw on that preparation by referring to evidence on the topic, text, or issue to probe and reflect on ideas under discussion. (SL.6.1a)

- Review the key ideas expressed and demonstrate understanding of multiple perspectives through reflection and paraphrasing. (SL.6.1d)

- Interpret information presented in diverse media and formats (e.g., visually, quantitatively, orally) and explain how it contributes to a topic, text, or issue under study. (SL.6.2)
- Delineate a speaker's argument and specific claims, distinguishing claims that are supported by reasons and evidence from claims that are not. (SL.6.3)
- Include multimedia components (e.g., graphics, images, music, sound) and visual displays in presentations to clarify information. (SL.6.5)

Skills, knowledge, and dispositions:

- SMART goal setting, tracking, adjusting, and reflecting
- Graph interpretation
- Nonfiction reading to determine the main idea
- Making an effective presentation
- Digital citizenship
- Grit or persistence
- Citing sources
- Employability skills
- Student success plans for after high school (such as résumé writing)

When deciding which common skills and concepts to focus on first as a team, ask yourself these two questions to guide your decision making.

1. "Which skills and concepts are *most* essential?" In other words, which ones have the highest degree of readiness and endurance, are assessed, and have leverage in other classes? Even when you deem something essential, it does not necessarily mean it is equally as essential.

2. "Which skills and concepts do I need the most support with?" In other words, prioritize the skills and concepts proven to be more difficult over the ones you have experienced greater success with.

In a specific unit, you might be teaching essentials you don't have in common while collaborating with your teammate on other essentials you do have in common at the same time. That's OK. Improvement is an ongoing, continuous process. You can't focus on improving everything at once. Remember, you eat an elephant one bite at a time.

A Note for Leaders: Providing Support

Collaboration on a course-alike team typically looks similar week to week and unit to unit; the team is teaching the same content at the same time. Team members are building common formative assessments together and always administering them using the same timeframe. Members work together to best respond to the students' learning needs. Leaders will observe these team actions over and over as the team completes instructional cycles.

A singleton common-content team does not look like this. Sometimes members use a common rubric for common content. Sometimes members apply this rubric together after they find opportunities to pace their curricula the same. However, sometimes one teacher will use the common rubric in October, and another teacher will use it in February. Then, there will be times when singletons are collaborating about non-common content, which we will cover in chapter 6 (page 87). This can change week to week and sometimes during a single collaborative team meeting. Rarely do two meetings look the same. Ensure singletons know you acknowledge this difference.

Many singleton teams will need support discovering what they have in common. These teams might initially think they have very little in common and prefer to remain working in isolation. Initially, one of the most powerful things you can do is to study their standards and provide teachers with some examples. It is very influential when you can walk into a team meeting and say, "I was briefly analyzing your standards yesterday, and I already discovered three skills you all teach. I can't wait to see what else you find you have in common."

Depending on the content areas of the teachers on the singleton team, most will need resources and support to build common rubrics. Providing professional development, which could consist of help from another collaborative team on the process of creating rubrics, might be needed. Begin to gather samples from other teams to share.

Finally, as you monitor and provide feedback to the team, constantly reassure members it is OK their team looks different from a traditional team. Ask members when they will finish identifying their common content, complete a common rubric, and utilize the rubric. After each of these critical steps, celebrate the team's accomplishments and reassure members they are on the right track. This feedback and coaching are invaluable, especially at the beginning.

Finally, if one or more of your teachers are members of teams consisting of members from other campuses, we recommend you focus on monitoring and providing feedback to your staff only. If the team is having difficulties adhering to its commitments, it might become necessary to connect with the administrators from the other school or schools to develop a plan to support the team.

Why Do It? Common-Content Teams

In our work in schools, we hear many reasons—or, more accurately, excuses—singleton teachers and leaders may have for not wanting to do the work of collaboration. Do any of these reasons resonate with you?

- **Reasons to Not Do the Work**
  - ▸ "It takes time to sit down and identify what essentials we have in common and to build common rubrics. It seems like a lot of work, and I'm already busy."
  - ▸ "Even when we identify what we have in common, there will still be content we don't have in common."
  - ▸ "Writing common rubrics is something new, and it creates feelings of being unsure. What if the rubrics aren't very good?"
  - ▸ "Having comparable data and someone looking at my data seems intimidating. Weaknesses might be exposed and used against us."
  - ▸ "These new tasks seem overwhelming, and we have to manage them as we continue to do what we have always done."
  - ▸ "It seems impossible for two teachers teaching different content to really help each other and make it worth their time."

While these questions and thoughts are real, the support and camaraderie you receive from working on a team are far superior. We've heard over and over educators say working on a team is the best decision they ever made. Many describe it as motivational and energizing. Take those first steps and discover the power of meaningful collaboration.

- **Reasons to Do the Work**
  - ▸ Identifying what essentials you have in common provides you with a support system you never knew you had and allows you to partner with colleagues at a deeper level.

▸ It will reduce those feelings of isolation and provide you with new avenues of ideas and problem solving.

▸ You will build clarity on what your standards say and what student proficiency looks like. This increased clarity will sharpen your instruction and allow you to better communicate expectations to your students.

▸ Students will begin to see how their learning in one class can impact the learning in another class. (For example, learning how to use mathematical representations in biology will help students when they enter chemistry the following year.)

▸ Having comparative data with a teammate is a game changer. Seeing each other's strengths and building on them are invigorating. Being able to ask, "Show me how you taught that" and then being able to use this new learning the very next day are powerful.

▸ Providing common rubrics to new staff members will accelerate their learning and build their clarity about student proficiency.

▸ Providing common rubrics along with exemplars allows you to engage your students at a deeper level and helps them build clarity on what you expect. Students are able to reflect and revise work more effectively.

Conclusion

In this second on-ramp, team members lay out their essential standards side by side with those of their collaborative team members. They identify the skills they teach, unit by unit, and compare them with their teammates'. There will be some common content. Teams pace content whenever possible and then begin to collaborate, avoiding isolation and benefitting from the expertise of other educators.

In the next chapter, you will learn how to collaborate about non-common content with the critical-friend on-ramp. As you establish common rubrics about the common content and become more proficient in the process, you will start finding more opportunities to collaborate about non-common content. However, remember to always prioritize your time with what you have in common.

Tools and Resources

Refer to these tools and resources to learn more about the content covered in this chapter.

We recommend the following resources that supplement the key concepts of the four critical PLC questions when a team is collaborating about common content.

- *How to Develop PLCs for Singletons and Small Schools* (Hansen, 2015, pp. 7–18, "Vertical Teams")
- *Simplifying Common Assessment* (Bailey & Jakicic, 2017, pp. 106–119, "Using Common Assessments With Singleton Teachers")

CHAPTER 6

Critical-Friend On-Ramp

*Don't get me wrong; any increased level of collaboration is
a good thing, and you have to start somewhere.*

—Aaron Hansen

Gary was the only technology elective teacher at his high school; his principal, Josh, asked him to collaborate with the other elective teachers while the
remaining teachers at the school collaborated with their course-alike team members.
Gary liked his elective department teammates (consisting of art, Spanish, and student leadership singletons), but he wasn't so sure how effectively they could help him
or how much he could help them. He knew creating and using formative assessments
were at the heart of the work of a collaborative team, but just about everything they
teach is different. He knew they should be discussing their instruction, but how does
that work when they are teaching different subjects? Gary wondered, "What do we
do together? What do we focus on?"

Josh was excited because all but a few staff members at his high school were on a
collaborative team and ready to go. He knew he shouldn't let any staff member opt
out of collaborating, but he was unsure of how to get his art teacher, Spanish teacher,
technology teacher, and student leadership teacher started. Fortunately, all four had
the same collaboration period, and now Josh needed to provide direction to get
them started. In previous discussions, Josh struggled to get the team to identify any

common curricula as a foundation for collaboration. His previous attempts to help all four find a virtual partner hadn't resulted in establishing a meaningful teammate yet. The four are willing, but they don't know how to make it happen.

Pause and Reflect

TEACHERS

- Can you transfer and use effective instructional strategies from a teacher in another content area in your classroom?
- Would it be helpful to get a teammate's eyes on your struggling students' work and listen to the teammate's ideas on how to best support the students' learning?

LEADERS

- In what ways could colleagues who don't teach the same subjects provide meaningful feedback to one another?
- What structures could you provide to singletons that would lead to meaningful collaboration?

If all educators are doing the most effective job they *know* how to do, how do they get better? The answer is actually quite simple: they must learn how to be more effective. The better question is, "How do I learn to be more effective?" Collaborative teacher teams are the building blocks of PLCs (DuFour et al., 2016). Collaborating with others (teachers with teachers, administrators with administrators, and so on) is what we call *job-embedded learning*. Collaboration is about analyzing and impacting how you do your job to better meet your students' learning needs. A critical friend can stimulate that learning.

Systems scientist and founder of the Society for Organizational Learning Peter M. Senge (1990), in his book *The Fifth Discipline,* captures the essence of team learning when he writes:

> The discipline of team learning involves mastering the practices of dialogue and discussion. The purpose of a dialogue is to go beyond any one individual's understanding. In dialogue, a group explores complex difficult issues from many points of view. (p. 224)

The role of a critical friend is to engage in dialogue and discussion so both partners can learn from each other, improving each other's individual knowledge and exploring teaching and learning from different points of view. As mentioned in chapter 2 (page 15), the critical-friend on-ramp is not the most effective way to improve teacher practices and learning for students and adults; therefore, this on-ramp should be seen as a temporary solution to the problem of isolation.

This chapter looks at the requirements for using the critical-friend on-ramp, including the requirements of a presenting teacher and a critical friend; how to tackle the four critical questions with a critical friend; guidance for leaders; and why forming critical-friend teams is worth doing.

Requirements When Using the Critical-Friend On-Ramp

When using the critical-friend on-ramp, the singleton team—composed of the presenting teacher and the critical friend (or friends)—must make specific commitments and take required actions as a team. In this type of collaboration, the singleton teacher brings a challenge or dilemma to the collaborative meeting with those fulfilling the role of critical friends. All members of the team should rotate taking the role of the presenting teacher. The challenge or dilemma (which we expand on in the next section) should directly relate to the four critical questions of a PLC. For example, "How should I respond to students when they haven't learned the essential learning?" and "What is the most effective way to assess the essential learning?"

First and foremost, the entire team must begin by building trust. Team members, especially the singleton bringing forth the challenge (the presenting teacher), must feel comfortable that the other team members will not judge them. When all members are clear that the intent of serving as a critical friend is to help, support, and explore more effective ways of meeting students' needs—not to judge one another—then team members will more likely be transparent and vulnerable with one another. Without this level of trust, team members might be reluctant to share challenges that expose a weakness, and they will not be in the mindset to listen and learn from others.

We find it helpful and effective for teams to adopt specific *data norms* when engaging in these critical-friend conversations. We use the term *data* not just to represent numbers but also other evidence of student learning, such as student work samples and student writing. Consider adopting data norms such as the following and reviewing them prior to entering into any critical-friend discussions or dialogue.

1. We will use evidence of student learning (data) to learn together.

2. We will refrain from using judgmental statements when dialoguing using evidence of student learning.

3. We will use evidence of student learning to help one another and our team improve.

4. We will use evidence of student learning to inform our team what to do next.

5. We will not make excuses about what the evidence of student learning tells our team.

Required Commitments of a Presenting Teacher

The teacher presenting the challenge to other team members serving as critical friends must prepare for the team discussion. If the presenting teacher is unprepared, the critical-friend teammates will become frustrated and eventually become disengaged and less willing to support their teammate. Following are the steps the singleton teacher takes when presenting the challenge and collaborating with critical friends.

STEP 1: IDENTIFY THE CHALLENGE

The presenting teacher must closely examine the evidence of student learning and determine what specific challenge best warrants the efforts and thoughts of his or her critical friends. When examining the student work, look for gaps between what you sought to have students show and what you are actually seeing. Ask yourself, "What am I seeing that I shouldn't see? What am I not seeing that I should see?" Determine your specific challenges by asking yourself the following types of questions.

- "Where did my students have the most difficulty demonstrating proficiency?"

- "In what part of the student learning does the evidence indicate my instructional strategies and approach were least effective?"

- "In what aspect of my students' learning difficulties do I feel least equipped to provide effective intervention and help them reach proficiency?"

As you ask yourself these questions and the challenge becomes clearer, collect several work samples that best illustrate the challenge you identify. This will help your teammates see what you are seeing.

For example, in this step, when examining the writing of English learners, the presenting teacher notices students are not incorporating the academic and content vocabulary the class learned as part of the unit. They know the vocabulary and have vocabulary notebooks, but it is not transferring to their writing.

STEP 2: DESCRIBE YOUR CURRENT REALITY

With a challenge identified, the presenting teacher should prepare to explain the essential standard or learning targets of the identified challenge to the critical-friend team. The presentation could consist of the deconstructed student-friendly learning targets, a rubric, proficient work exemplars, or any other artifacts that will help build shared understanding of the expected learning outcome.

Next, the presenting teacher should prepare to share how he or she initially taught the students. This gives context to critical friends before engaging in dialogue and exploring new ideas. The presenting teacher could consider bringing a copy of the anchor chart, graphic organizers, and pictures from the classroom showing the presenting teacher using specific instructional approaches. Bring to the team meeting any evidence that will effectively and efficiently help the team members understand how the presenting teacher initially taught the content.

For example, in step 2, the presenting teacher shares the writing of five English learners along with the vocabulary notebooks of the same five students. The teacher highlights in each piece of writing where the students could have used the taught vocabulary to strengthen their writing according to the writing rubric. The presenting teacher then shows the team members how he or she taught the vocabulary and instructed students to use their notebooks while writing.

STEP 3: DRAFT SPECIFIC QUESTIONS

Often when examining student work and comparing nonproficient work alongside proficient work, specific questions may come to mind.

- "Why are my English learners struggling with the concept and not other students?"
- "How might I utilize other modalities to improve learning?"
- "In what ways could I increase student engagement in this challenging concept?"

Presenting teachers should write down these questions and share them when presenting the challenge to the team. Sharing these questions will help guide the discussion and lead to specific ideas and suggestions. The overall goal of the presenting teacher is to help the critical friends best understand the challenge or dilemma and provide them the opportunity to give suggestions and ideas to improve student learning. The feedback the presenting teacher needs must be specific and actionable.

Continuing with the English learners example, in step 3, the presenting teacher is seeking answers to questions such as the following.

- Do students actually know the vocabulary, or are they just completing the vocabulary notebook as instructed?

- How could I better model for students how to use their vocabulary notebook when they are independently writing?

- What is the best way to give students feedback about their writing? Do I give them feedback during or after they complete their writing?

Required Commitments of a Critical Friend

Not only does the presenting teacher need to prepare but also do those serving as critical friends. Among the greatest challenges critical friends face are having an open mind and practicing active listening skills. These can prove challenging if the team is meeting after a long day of teaching or if the critical-friend teammates themselves are facing many challenges. It requires a sincere desire and discipline to help teammates. The following steps outline the requirements of being a critical friend for a colleague.

STEP 1: CLEAR YOUR MIND AND BE PREPARED TO ACTIVELY LISTEN

To successfully support a colleague, a critical friend needs to understand the presenting teacher's dilemma, the situation, and what the teacher needs support with. This requires carefully listening and fully engaging in what the teacher is presenting. It will be difficult, if not impossible, for someone to act as a critical friend if he or she does not have a clear understanding of the presenting teacher's specific situation. To continue the example from the previous section, in this step, the critical friend takes notes while the presenting teacher describes the challenge. The critical friend circles examples of the challenge when looking at the student writing samples.

STEP 2: WRITE DOWN CLARIFICATION QUESTIONS WHILE THE PRESENTING TEACHER IS DESCRIBING THE CHALLENGE AND CURRENT REALITY

As the presenting teacher explains the current situation, the critical friend should write down questions while seeking to understand the challenge. For example, in this step, a critical friend might note the following questions.

- Do you see any of your English learners transferring the vocabulary to their writing? If so, could you ask them what helped them?

- Do your students have their notebooks open while writing?

- Do you have an anchor chart that guides students in using their notebook?

- When teaching the vocabulary, how do you determine if students know the vocabulary?

STEP 3: SEEK TO UNDERSTAND THE PRESENTER'S CURRENT REALITY THROUGH DIALOGUE AND DISCUSSION

When the presenting teacher has completed sharing the dilemma and situation, the critical friend needs the opportunity to ask clarifying questions. (This is when you ask the questions you jotted down in the previous step.) As with most communication, new questions may emerge. Continue to engage in this dialogue and discussion until you have the clarity to provide feedback and ideas. To continue the example, the conversation in this step might occur as follows.

> Critical friend: "Do you have an anchor chart posted to support students in using their vocabulary notebook?"
>
> Presenting teacher: "No, but I tell them to get out their notebooks and use them."
>
> Critical friend: "Do you use anchor charts for any other standards? Do they work?"
>
> Presenting teacher: "Yes, I just used one in the last unit when teaching citing textual evidence."
>
> Critical friend: "Did you see students using the anchor chart? Did it help them in the last unit?"

STEP 4: SHARE RELEVANT EXPERIENCES AND IDEAS

Toward the end of the discussion, the presenting teacher will ask for the critical friends' best thinking and ideas regarding the challenge. Critical friends should draw on their experiences and knowledge to provide input and best thinking, responding to the following types of questions.

- Have you ever encountered a similar situation?

- Based on your knowledge and experiences, what did you find successful that might help the presenting teacher?

- Based on your knowledge and experiences, what did you find unsuccessful? What might the presenting teacher avoid in the current situation?

- What resources or materials might you share to support the presenting teacher in the current situation?

Please note, the timeframe of these steps will vary depending on the complexity of the presenting teacher's challenge or dilemma. In general, teams should complete all steps in no more than thirty minutes.

The PLC Critical Questions on a Critical-Friend Team

Once the steps of presenting and discussing a challenge are complete, the critical-friend team can move on to answering the four critical questions of a PLC.

CRITICAL QUESTION ONE

Working with a critical friend to answer the first critical question of a PLC, "What knowledge, skills, and dispositions should every student acquire as a result of this unit, this course, or this grade level?" (DuFour et al., 2016, p. 36), can help presenting teachers better focus and understand what they determined essential and develop the most effective instructional units and lessons. Dialoguing and discussing the planning and preparing for an upcoming unit or lesson most often lead presenting teachers to further refine and improve their work.

First, presenting teachers should ensure the instructional time they allotted during a unit aligns with what they determined essential. Some essential learning may be more essential than others. For example, most teachers would agree that a kindergarten student learning his letters and the letters' corresponding sounds is of the utmost importance—more essential than recognizing and producing rhyming words (although those also might be essential). Another powerful aspect of addressing the first critical question is to ensure teachers maintain the rigor of the language of the standards. We sometimes find isolated teachers unintentionally misaligning the actual standard and student-friendly learning targets. For example, the standard states students should *describe*, but the learning target uses the verb *identify*. The critical friend can provide this feedback and help correct the misalignment before any instruction on the standard.

A significant component of the critical-friend discussion should focus on instruction. Enhance planning effective instruction by anticipating the skills and concepts most difficult for students. This is when past experience in the classroom is beneficial. As the well-known proverb says, "Experience is the best teacher." It is helpful to consider your past experiences and what caused previous students difficulty and seek additional or new approaches. For newer teachers, experienced critical friends can share their insights. Another avenue to refining your instructional plan is to consider others on campus who have expertise in the skill or concept you are planning to teach. Consider them informal critical friends. An informal critical friend might be a staff member in another grade level, department, or possibly another building. Teachers should use informal critical friends in addition to their collaborative team members. Figure 6.1 provides a template to use in this on-ramp when addressing PLC critical question one.

Critical-Friend Template for PLC Critical Question One

Unit: _____

Date: _____

A critical friend and a presenting teacher engage in a collaborative conversation by asking and discussing these items when planning an upcoming instructional unit or series of lessons.

1. What are your essentials and learning targets in this unit of study or lesson?

2. When examining the standards and learning targets in this unit, which ones do you anticipate being the most difficult for students to reach proficiency? How might you utilize more instructional time on these anticipated aspects of the unit or lesson?

3. What strategies, activities, and resources will you use to support student learning? Do you believe these will be sufficient to ensure learning or are additional strategies, activities, and resources needed?

4. How might I help you? Is there someone else on the campus who might have strategies and resources that would benefit your planning?

FIGURE 6.1: Critical-friend template for PLC critical question one.
*Visit **go.SolutionTree.com/PLCbooks** to download a reproducible version of this figure.*

CRITICAL QUESTION TWO

PLC critical question two asks teachers to reflect: "How will we know when each student has acquired the essential knowledge and skills?" (DuFour et al., 2016, p. 36). Critical-friend teams or partners can be extremely helpful in evaluating the response for singletons.

Formatively assessing your students throughout and at the end of the unit will provide you with the information to be agile in your instruction. The design and use of formative assessments are critical to provide both accurate and timely information. We recommend beginning the dialogue and discussion by asking yourself the following three questions.

1. "What information will I need to ensure no student gets left behind during this unit?"

2. "When will I need each piece of information?"

3. "What is the most effective and efficient way to get this information for each student?"

As consultant and speaker Nicole Dimich (2015) writes in her book *Design in Five*, "The intent of a formative assessment is to provide results that a teacher can use to plan a lesson in which students fix their mistakes or revise their work" (p. 37).

Crucial components of PLC question two are to ensure your assessments match the rigor of the essential learning and the information you gather is valid for making instructional decisions. Discussing the complexity of thinking in the essentials (and listing them in the learning targets) helps ensure your assessments match. Using Webb's Depth of Knowledge (DOK) to identify the level of thinking in the standards and targets helps ensure rigor. Singletons, since they are often designing assessments alone, may rely more on publisher assessments or banks of assessment items that may not be at the rigor level of the standard. Therefore, we recommend paying special attention to ensure a match in the DOK level with the essential learning and assessment. Also, the assessment must match the content. It is vital to revisit the verbs in the essential standards and learning targets to ensure the assessment matches (see chapter 3, page 29). If the standard asks students to *describe*, the assessment must ask students to *describe*. When you match the content and rigor of the essentials, you ensure valid data. Figure 6.2 provides a template you can use as you address PLC critical question two.

CRITICAL QUESTIONS THREE AND FOUR

PLC critical questions three and four ask teachers to consider, "How will we respond when some students do not learn?" and "How will we extend the learning for students who are already proficient?" (DuFour et al., 2016, p. 36). Critical-friend teams or partners can be extremely helpful in evaluating the response for singletons.

Assessments are neither summative nor formative; rather, you *use* an assessment either summatively or formatively. The formative assessment process of using the newly acquired information about your students' current learning to modify your teaching and continue their learning is indispensable to meeting the needs of all students. Discussion and collaboration with a critical friend about the best ways to respond when initial instruction does not provide the results hoped for allow teachers to enhance both student and adult learning.

Critical-Friend Template for PLC   Unit: _____
Critical Question Two

Date: _____

A critical friend and a teacher engage in a collaborative conversation by asking and discussing these items when planning an upcoming formative assessment.

1. How do you plan to formatively assess students throughout the unit and provide actionable feedback?

2. When looking at the language, especially the verbs of the standard and learning targets, does the level of thinking on the assessment align to the standard and learning targets? For example, if the standard asks students to *compare*, do assessment items ask students to *compare*?

3. Does the DOK level (complexity of thinking) of the assessment items match the DOK level of the standard and targets?

4. In reading the prompts and assessment items, is the assessment clearly written? Will students understand what you want them to do?

5. Will the data you receive from the assessment provide specific information that enables you to diagnose and provide meaningful interventions for students' learning needs? Will you be able to provide specific feedback to the students to further their learning?

6. Are there enough data?

7. Does the design of the assessments align to high-stakes tests students will encounter?

8. Does the assessment ask students to explain their thinking and reasoning to best understand their level of proficiency?

FIGURE 6.2: Critical-friend template for PLC critical question two.
*Visit **go.SolutionTree.com/PLCbooks** to download a reproducible version of this figure.*

The critical-friend conversation about the third critical question begins by closely examining the evidence of student learning. This obviously involves analyzing the formative assessment the team utilized in answering question two, but it should also involve analyzing other student work leading up to the formative assessment. It is much like being a detective. Teachers are not only trying to figure out specifically what students have and haven't learned to target what they need but also discover what did and didn't work to help students learn. Knowing not all students learn the same way, this close examination of what did and didn't work during initial core instruction allows the discussion with critical friends to focus on new or revised strategies. Rarely does simply repeating ineffective strategies result in the desired student learning.

Teachers and teams often struggle with planning and implementing instruction about critical question four due to a lack of preplanning. Teachers often spend the majority of their time after formatively assessing on planning interventions, but how to extend learning gets ignored. We find the best approach to planning for extending learning is to plan the instruction prior to beginning the unit. Anticipate students being ready to have their learning extended when you assess. Therefore, plan in advance. Here are three common ways to extend learning.

1. Plan instruction that asks students to apply the essential skills or concept at a higher level of thinking (DOK level).

2. Plan instruction that asks students to engage with more complex text.

3. Plan instruction about grade-level standards not identified as essential and, therefore, not part of your core instructional plan.

Figure 6.3 provides a template teachers can use as they address PLC questions three and four.

Perspectives From the Field

When I first heard the acronym *PLC* (professional learning community) on my first day at Harrisburg Middle School, I admit I rolled my eyes. I tried to keep an open mind, however, and be receptive to this idea of working in a different way as a music teacher. When the actual work began, I was pleasantly surprised. The PLC process actually allowed me to examine my content standards and state-mandated structures and determine the essential learning from those. I began doing this work by myself, as I was the only one who taught the same music classes at Harrisburg. During the year of PLC implementation, I further examined the structures for my music classes. I determined the essential skills music students need as a foundation for music learning, including reading music. Reading music begins with rhythmic skills—both reading and performing rhythmic patterns. As I unpacked those essentials, I was able to determine how to teach and assess them. Here is when my critical friend came in handy.

As I wrote the skills, my critical friend, Landon, who does not teach music, analyzed my work and helped hone the language of my essential standards so that people, including students, who did not know my content could understand them. In addition, because my critical friend taught the same grade level, we shared the same students and could discuss modifications we might need for special needs students, as well as anticipated student behavioral needs that would help with planning lessons for a range of different learners.

—**Bill W., singleton music teacher**

Critical-Friend Template for PLC Critical Questions Three and Four

Unit: _____

Date: _____

A critical friend and a teacher engage in a collaborative conversation by asking and discussing these items as part of analyzing the data and evidence from a recent formative assessment and planning interventions and extensions.

1. Share a breakdown of proficiency by student and by skill. What areas of strength do the data reveal? What areas of concern?

2. How might you organize your instruction using common mistakes or misconceptions?

3. What is your plan for students who have and have not learned the essential standard? When will you provide the additional time and support?

4. What changes will you make to your instruction based on these struggles? What did you learn?

5. What ideas or suggestions can you provide as a critical friend?

6. How will you reassess student learning?

7. How will you extend learning for those who demonstrate mastery? How can you increase the level of thinking? How can you utilize text of increased complexity? Should you engage students in learning grade-level nonessential content?

8. In what ways could letting parents know of their child's progress on the essentials help the situation?

FIGURE 6.3: Critical-friend template for PLC critical questions three and four.

*Visit **go.SolutionTree.com/PLCbooks** to download a reproducible version of this figure.*

A Note for Leaders: Providing Support

Leaders often face the hurdle of singleton team members building trust and being vulnerable with one another. These teams might come from different content areas and have different interests. We find one of the most effective strategies for building trust is for a leader to encourage one team member to model vulnerability by exposing a difficulty and asking for help. Often, when one person models this vulnerability, a second member reciprocates. Another way a leader can build trust is to ensure team members engage in creating team norms that promote trust.

Leaders should discuss the critical-friend templates in this chapter. At the beginning, as a team utilizes the templates, building trust might take longer than anticipated. Leaders can observe the implementation of the templates and provide feedback. It is important for leaders to reassure teams, especially at the beginning.

One of the most effective ways a leader can support the work is to explicitly point out and celebrate the increase in learning that results from a team engaging in a critical-friend conversation. When a leader walks into a classroom and sees a singleton teacher implementing a new strategy learned from the critical friend, praise him or her for being a learner. Then walk right over to the critical friend's room and let that teacher know what you just saw and thank him or her for sharing his or her best thinking. Acknowledging how the critical-friend discussion impacts the classroom for the better lets the involved teachers know you value their collaborative time. Most of all, look for how students' learning increases because of these conversations in collaborative team meetings. If a team member revises an assessment based on input from a critical friend, the result being access to more reliable data, point it out. Teachers want to be successful. Point out their critical-friend actions are leading to greater success. When teams experience their collaboration working, they will continue to do it. Continue to look for changes in the classroom linked to team collaboration. Accomplish this by reviewing collaborative team meeting notes and looking for implementation success. Lack of change in a classroom is symptomatic of ineffective collaboration. When this happens, the leader should more closely examine the collaboration to ensure the team members are reflecting, seeking to improve, and implementing knowledge they gain during team meetings.

Why Do It? Critical-Friend Teams

In our work in schools, we hear many reasons—or, more accurately, excuses—singleton teachers and leaders may have for not wanting to do the work of collaboration. Do any of these reasons resonate with you?

- **Reasons to Not Do the Work**
  - ▸ "It is simpler to plan and teach my content without the help of anyone else."
  - ▸ "It is stressful to share my results and let my colleagues know what is not going well."
  - ▸ "My students are my students, and it is not my responsibility to help other teachers."
  - ▸ "I've been working in isolation for years, and my results have been fine."

We encourage you to remember that it's possible to increase individual and collective knowledge by learning together. It can be difficult to shift away from working in isolation, but the ability and benefits of learning from others outweigh any difficulties.

- **Reasons to Do the Work**
  - ▸ Your teammate might have the best idea to help you with something you struggle with.
  - ▸ It is very gratifying when you help a colleague get better.
  - ▸ Knowing you have a collaborative team that can help you and provide different perspectives helps reduce the feeling of isolation.
  - ▸ Working interdependently with your collaborative team reduces the stress of trying to solve problems all by yourself.
  - ▸ Using a template of questions specifically designed for a critical friend enhances your discussions and increases your individual and collective learning.

Conclusion

Isolation and the status quo are the enemies of continuous improvement. When a teacher is the only one teaching a specific grade, course, or content different from anyone else, a critical friend can provide the support and ideas a singleton teacher needs to overcome challenges.

In the next chapter, we provide some key guidance for leaders on how to help singletons avoid working in isolation and engage in meaningful collaboration. It is important to develop a process to monitor and coach your singleton teams while keeping the work doable.

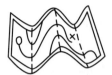

Tools and Resources

Refer to these tools and resources to learn more about the content covered in this chapter.

We recommend the following resources that supplement the key concepts about the four PLC critical questions when a singleton is collaborating with a critical friend.

- *Design in Five* (Dimich, 2015, pp. 120–121, Consider Instruction Based on Readiness)

- *Simplifying Common Assessment* (Bailey & Jakicic, 2017, pp. 33–36, Identify the Role of Rigor in the Standards)

- *Essential Assessment* (Erkens, Schimmer, & Dimich, 2017, pp. 104–107, Instructional Agility in the Classroom)

CHAPTER 7

Putting It All Together

*When school leaders work with their staffs to
create a timeline for anticipated products, it helps
teams focus on the work to be done.*

—Richard DuFour and Robert J. Marzano

Martin was feeling pretty good about the PLC process at Scenic Elementary where he served as principal. The grade-level teams were established, and the special education teachers were each part of the teams that most matched their caseloads. The music teacher had found another music teacher across town with whom to collaborate virtually, and the physical education teacher was going to prepare for future meaningful collaboration on her own with the help of a teacher coach at Scenic. With the teams in place and protected time established for each teacher to do the work expected, Martin now turned his attention to what his responsibilities would be now that the singletons in his school were situated in appropriate collaborative relationships. How would he monitor teams and know if the teachers were being successful? What would he do if singletons resisted collaboration? What could he do to celebrate success?

Pause and Reflect

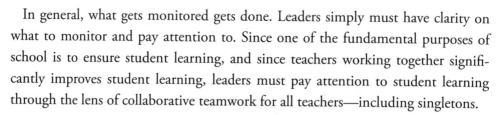

LEADERS

- What are indicators that a team or a singleton needs support?
- In what ways could you monitor the work of teams and singletons?

In general, what gets monitored gets done. Leaders simply must have clarity on what to monitor and pay attention to. Since one of the fundamental purposes of school is to ensure student learning, and since teachers working together significantly improves student learning, leaders must pay attention to student learning through the lens of collaborative teamwork for all teachers—including singletons.

The work of collaboration doesn't always go smoothly. Collaboration as it occurs in the PLC process is a new concept for most educators as well as school leaders. It can become overwhelming if a leader doesn't know how to organize the teams and singletons on campus. The on-ramps help leaders understand how to organize teams. This clarity helps leaders from being overwhelmed and promotes step-by-step implementation. Even with the best planning, leaders will still encounter resistance, but a plan for moving forward in spite of resistance helps. Utilizing the on-ramps helps leaders and teachers know how to do the work in meaningful ways, reducing resistance.

This chapter puts it all together by exploring some necessary shifts in the leaders' work when singleton teachers collaborate: the products leaders must monitor, how leaders can keep the work doable, and how to deal with resistance.

Monitoring Team Products

We recommend starting with a spreadsheet to track what each team has and has not yet created. The far-left column of figure 7.1 shows every team on campus, as well as singletons who may or may not yet have a meaningful collaborative partner. In the next column to the right are the team norms, which leaders should be aware of. If every team submits norms except one, this product-tracking spreadsheet will easily identify which team needs more time and support for this task. As singletons are working to find meaningful collaboration, those singletons who haven't found a

Teams and Singletons	Norms	First Essential Learning	SMART Goal	Formative Assessment	Action Plan	Final Percent of Students Proficient on Essential Learning
Algebra 1 team	Yes	Yes	Yes	No	No	58
English 10 team	Yes	Yes	Yes	Yes	Yes	77
World history team	Yes	Yes	No	No	No	Unknown
Computer teacher	No	Yes	Yes	Yes	Yes	82
Band teacher	No	Yes	Yes	Yes	No	71
Technology teacher	Yes	Yes	Yes	Yes	Yes	93

FIGURE 7.1: Example of a PLC product tracker for school leadership teams.

Visit go.SolutionTree.com/PLCbooks to download a reproducible version of this figure.

partner yet, and therefore haven't developed norms, could also receive more time and support to locate their on-ramp on the journey of finding meaningful collaboration.

The next column identifies the first essential learning, then the SMART goal for that essential learning, followed by the common formative assessment the team plans to use to determine which students are proficient in the essential learning and which students need more time and support. Teams then create their action plans after analyzing the formative assessment results.

Some leaders find it valuable to track the percent of students proficient with the essential learning using this tool as well (far-right column). In addition, if the tracking spreadsheet includes hyperlinked products, teams can view the products other teams are creating.

During their initial attempts to collaborate, teams composed entirely of singletons or that include singleton members will need guiding templates or protocols. Eventually teachers become skilled enough in the PLC process to use a shortened protocol, such as the one-page summary of the PLC process in figure 7.2.

We find that without protocols (templates), teams struggle to follow the PLC process and can inadvertently skip critical steps. But beware, however, that protocols are not enough: "Simply providing the protocol is a good start, but it is essential that you work through a protocol with the team initially to explain the purpose and walk them through the process to ensure effective use" (Spiller & Power, 2019, p. 28).

If a leader makes copies of the protocols or sends them out electronically to a team's members, with a note saying, "Turn these in," those team members are likely to see the protocols as "one more thing" to do. But the intent of any protocol is to stimulate the critical conversations teacher teams must have to improve student learning, not to simply fill out the protocols (templates) and turn them in. The journey *is* the destination. It has no end point, but is instead a cycle of continuous improvement. Often teachers and leaders are familiar with the four critical questions of the PLC process, however, the details of on-ramps often represent new learning on school campuses. These new concepts typically require leaders to take the time to work through the protocols alongside singletons to answer questions, learn together, and encourage them.

Team:			
Collaborative Team Guide for a Unit of Study Purpose: Increase student learning and capture adult learning.			
INFORMATION TEAM AGREES ON PRIOR TO TEACHING THE UNIT			
Unit title and essential number:	Begin date:	End date:	Number of instructional days:
Common formative assessment (CFA) date (before end date) (Link to CFA)	Date to establish inter-rater reliability:	Date to share results and build action plan:	Dates for interventions and extensions:
What is the essential (standard)?			
What is the team SMART goal?			
ACTION PLAN TEAM DETERMINES AFTER THE CFA			
List (or link to) students who need more time and support (percent not yet proficient)			
How will teachers give support, and what is the timeline for this support?			
What is the extension plan for students who are already proficient?			
REFLECTIONS TEAM CAPTURES AFTER CARRYING OUT THE ACTION PLAN			
What percent of students is currently proficient after the action plan?			
After interventions, did the team meet the SMART goal?			
What intervention strategies proved most effective?			
What research-based best practices got the best results? Capture changes to initial instruction the team needs to make in this unit or in future units and any other team learning.			
What is the plan for students who still haven't learned this essential?			

Copyright © 2021 by Brig Leane. Used with permission.

FIGURE 7.2: Collaborative team guide for a unit of study.

*Visit **go.SolutionTree.com/PLCbooks** to download a reproducible version of this figure.*

Pause and Reflect

- How do teachers know what matters to the school administration?
- How will leaders know which teams need more time and support?
- In what ways are teacher teams receiving feedback on their PLC products?
- In what ways could leaders give feedback to teams on the PLC products they generate?
- What next steps are you considering?

Keeping It Doable

We know teachers are not sitting around waiting for tasks to occupy their idle time. They are busy, and their plates are full. While the idea of having singletons find meaningful collaboration makes sense, it can seem overwhelming for already busy educators. We recommend starting small and moving forward as educators increase their knowledge and capacity for the changes we suggest. Some schools start by deciding all teams will answer the four critical questions of a PLC for at least one essential skill in an upcoming quarter to work through the PLC process. This allows teams to get some experience ensuring clarity of an essential skill, assessing to see if learning occurred, and doing something about it for students who have and have not demonstrated their learning of that essential. Teams who are ready to work through the process on more than one essential standard should do so, but only at a capacity they can handle given all their other expectations. Determining a singleton's capacity can often be as simple as asking, "Is the plan we created doable given your current situation?"

Leaders can track work and celebrate successes as teams move through the questions in the PLC process. Celebrating quick wins lets the staff know the importance of the work, and by showing the products teams are producing, leaders provide exemplars for other teams to learn from. For example, a leader could use figure 7.2 (page 107) to track the work of teams and singletons as they collaborate. Acknowledge teachers as they are working through the PLC process. This doesn't have to be complicated. It can be as simple as the leader walking into a team meeting and thanking members or putting a comment on a team's Google Doc. Showing exemplary team products to the whole staff is a good way to not only celebrate the hard work of teachers but also provide examples of success for other teachers and teams.

If a school doesn't have time in the master schedule for teachers to collaborate, it is unfair to expect teams to simply do this additional work; therefore, it is imperative that leaders carve out time for collaboration or remove something from teachers' plates before adding collaboration. Creating time for singletons to do this work is no different than creating time for any other team. We recommend DuFour and colleagues' (2016) guidebook, *Learning by Doing* (pp. 64–67) for excellent suggestions for finding collaboration time.

Dealing With Resistance

Over the years, many new ideas have come and gone in education. Each wave of change that came and then faded took energy with it, and experienced teachers have seen this happen over and over, leading many to feel the best way to maintain the energy they need for the incredibly demanding job is to simply shut their doors and teach. The educational establishment has earned the resistance teachers have when they hear of new programs to improve schools. It wouldn't be uncommon to hear things such as, "I don't have enough time," "We don't have anything in common, so this PLC stuff doesn't apply to me," or "This isn't going to help me as a singleton."

Knowing resistance will be a part of this change process can be very helpful. While the complexities of resistance and cultural change are too much to tackle in this book, Muhammad and Cruz (2019) outline the following four critical behaviors leaders should adopt to positively transform school culture.

1. **Communicate the rationale for change:** If staff members don't know why you expect them to change, there is an increased risk for resistance.

2. **Establish trust:** Trust is more important than likability. Trust requires character and competency. If educators trust their leader, they are less likely to resist change.

3. **Build capacity:** Teaching others how to work through the PLC process using protocols (templates) gives teams and educators the skills they need to be successful.

4. **Expect accountability for getting the right work done:** Leaders must make a gradual shift from supporting teams to expecting teams to engage in the PLC process.

Additionally, before beginning this process, leaders should think about the need to sustain the journey over the long haul and consider the timing of starting such a journey. Without this long-term mindset, the PLC process could end up as just another wave that came through the school, which took more energy, and when abandoned, left even more teachers with even greater resistance to future necessary change to meet the increasingly challenging task of educating all students. With clarity about the on-ramps for singletons, leaders can better assess the needs of their singletons and provide guidance toward meaningful collaboration.

Celebrating

Teachers don't have to wonder for long what matters at their schools; they can tell by what leaders celebrate, what leaders confront when the work is incomplete or doesn't succeed, what leaders discuss or ask questions about at the team level and as part of whole-school collaboration, what leaders fund, and the amount of time leaders set aside for certain activities. Leaders who want the PLC process to be the driving force for student and educator learning in their schools simply must make it clear to all staff what matters by their actions. Part of these efforts means ensuring the work of singletons and their various team configurations are visible parts of the schoolwide PLC process. In what ways are leaders showing what matters?

Think about an upcoming staff meeting. Imagine the staff meeting opens with a quick review of the school mission, and the main part of your mission focuses specifically on how your school is working to ensure learning for *all* students. Following this review, you like to have celebrations. What better celebrations to use than those aimed at ensuring learning for *all* students? We encourage you to celebrate singleton teachers who successfully determine an essential for a grade or course. Celebrate the short, common formative assessment a singleton team creates to determine whether students learned an essential standard. The exemplars teacher teams submit are easy to share. The effective principal shares the best of what singleton team members submit, just as they share the successful products of other grade- and course-level teams, highlighting exemplary parts of the products. Such celebrations act as encouragement to the teams that submit the products and give other teams insights into ways to create their team products.

Using Planning Checklists

To recap the many ideas woven throughout this book, we created figure 7.3 to help busy educators with steps to move the PLC process forward. Some of the items on the checklist apply to traditional collaborative teams, and some are specific to singletons. Consider customizing the checklist for your specific situation.

Teacher Planning Checklist

- ☐ Do I have dedicated time to collaborate?
- ☐ Do I have one or more partners with whom to collaborate?
- ☐ Do my partners and I have the best possible on-ramp?
- ☐ Do I know where to begin looking for a potential collaborative team member who shares the same subject I teach?
- ☐ Do I have and understand the templates (protocols) that pertain to my on-ramp to guide collaboration?
- ☐ Do I know the essential learning for the classes I teach?
- ☐ Have I made the essential learning clear to students using student-friendly language?
- ☐ Do I have a way to assess whether students learned the essential standards?
- ☐ Do I have a calendar of when the essential learning, as well as interventions for students who haven't yet learned those essentials, fit into a school year?
- ☐ Do I have a plan for when students don't demonstrate learning of an essential?
- ☐ Do I have a plan for extending the learning for students who demonstrate proficiency on an essential?

FIGURE 7.3: Teacher planning checklist.

*Visit **go.SolutionTree.com/PLCbooks** to download a reproducible version of this figure.*

Use figure 7.4 to assist in considering the leader's steps to move the PLC process forward for all school collaborative teams, including singleton teams.

Leader Planning Checklist

- ☐ Have I reinforced the need for collaboration with singletons and other teachers?
- ☐ Do I know which teachers are on which teams?
- ☐ Is the construction of teams meaningful?
- ☐ Is every teacher part of a collaborative team?
- ☐ Is time available during the workday for collaboration?
- ☐ Are the PLC product expectations clear for teams, including singleton teams?
- ☐ Have I shared the templates and tools of different on-ramps with singletons?
- ☐ Does the leadership team provide feedback on PLC products to teams and singletons?
- ☐ Does the whole staff celebrate exemplary team or singleton PLC products?
- ☐ Do I encourage singletons to find meaningful collaboration with others?
- ☐ Do I track the PLC products of teams and singletons to know which teachers need more time and support?

FIGURE 7.4: Leader planning checklist.

*Visit **go.SolutionTree.com/PLCbooks** to download a reproducible version of this figure.*

Why Do It? Singleton Teams in a PLC

In our work in schools, we hear many reasons—or, more accurately, excuses—singleton teachers and leaders may have for not wanting to do the work of collaboration. Do any of these reasons resonate with you?

- **Reasons to Not Do the Work**
  - ▸ "Leaders are already so busy with so many things to monitor, they just don't have the time or energy to track even one more good thing."
  - ▸ "Teams should have autonomy to produce what they want—standardization takes away from team creativity and flexibility."
  - ▸ "If leaders track PLC products, then teachers might feel bad if they were not completing the expected products—and teachers' main job is to teach—not to do paperwork."

The purpose of school is for all students to learn at high levels. Leaders must keep this mission foremost in the minds of everyone at the school. If leaders and teams don't track PLC products, the implication is that learning isn't the priority.

- **Reasons to Do the Work**
  - ▸ By tracking team products, it is easier to know which teams need more time and support.
  - ▸ By collecting (and celebrating high-quality) team products, leaders can showcase exemplars that help other teacher teams know what quality PLC work looks like.
  - ▸ Teams have access to the PLC products of other teams, thereby increasing cross-team collaboration.

Conclusion

The importance of leadership in the PLC process cannot be overstated. We have yet to see a school make the transformation from isolation to a PLC that extends to all teachers on campus without strong leadership. The more singletons, the more important leadership is, because leaders can't expect singletons to figure out the PLC process on their own without the delicate balance of support, guidance, and celebration with accountability. Keys are to keep the work doable and know that the ongoing PLC process is not a sprint, but a marathon.

Tools and Resources

Refer to these tools and resources to learn more about the content covered in this chapter.

We recommend the following resources that supplement the key concepts of addressing conflict and resistance and utilizing the power of celebrations.

- *Learning by Doing* (DuFour et al., 2016, pp. 211–219)
- *School Improvement for All* (Kramer & Schuhl, 2017, pp. 27–40)

Final Thoughts

Teachers won't be able to meet the needs of all their students if they continue to work in isolation. Even though many teachers don't have a natural course-alike partner in the same building, those teachers can still have meaningful collaboration. Collaboration that impacts student and teacher learning won't happen overnight, but it can happen, and it is our hope this book provides you with additional clarity on the pathway to making it happen. Teachers can choose among the different on-ramps, but the key is to start.

Singleton collaboration takes effort, but three fourth-grade teachers or a pair of high school biology teachers require similar effort to collaborate if they are used to working in isolation. Just because there are adults who teach the same subject working at the same school does not mean they will collaborate in ways that impact student and adult learning. Meaningful collaboration doesn't magically happen—it requires structure, focus, and a willingness on the part of team members each to work for the best interests of those they serve—the students. Becoming a PLC is a proven path.

Remember, a PLC is the larger organization: a school or a district committed to ensuring all students learn at high levels in a collaborative culture, with a relentless focus on student learning translating into better results. It is not a meeting of a team of teachers on a campus, something that can cause singletons to feel left out. Becoming a PLC is a way of thinking that *every* educator on a campus keeps foremost in their minds. Educators in a PLC continuously focus on increasing their clarity of what they want students to learn, how they will know if students have learned it, and what they will do if students don't learn it or already know it. Our hope is that singletons implement these ideas and gain more clarity on ways to collaborate in meaningful ways.

In a PLC, every educator counts!

References and Resources

Arkansas Department of Education. (2016a). *Arkansas K–12 Science Standards: Biology—Integrated.* Little Rock, AR: Author. Accessed at https://dese.ade.arkansas.gov/Files/20201211135825_Biology_Integrated_2016.pdf on February 19, 2022.

Arkansas Department of Education. (2016b). *Arkansas K–12 Science Standards: Chemistry—Integrated.* Little Rock, AR: Author. Accessed at https://dese.ade.arkansas.gov/Files/20201211135527_Chemistry_Integrated_2016.pdf on March 14, 2022.https://dese.ade.arkansas.gov/Files/20201211135825_Biology_Integrated_2016.pdf on February 19, 2022.

Bailey, K., & Jakicic, C. (2017). *Simplifying common assessment: A guide for Professional Learning Communities at Work.* Bloomington, IN: Solution Tree Press.

Brown, T., & Ferriter, W. M. (2021). *You can learn! Building student ownership, motivation, and efficacy with the PLC at Work process.* Bloomington, IN: Solution Tree Press.

Buffum, A., Mattos, M., & Malone, J. (2018). *Taking action: A handbook for RTI at Work.* Bloomington, IN: Solution Tree Press.

California Department of Education. (2000, May). *History–Social science content standards for California Public Schools: Kindergarten through grade twelve.* Sacramento, CA: Author. Accessed at https://cde.ca.gov/be/st/ss/documents/histsocscistnd.pdf on February 19, 2022.

California Department of Education. (2013a, March). *California Common Core State Standards: English language arts & literacy in history/social studies, science, and technical subjects.* Sacramento, CA: Author. Accessed at https://cde.ca.gov/be/st/ss/documents/finalelaccssstandards.pdf on February 19, 2022.

California Department of Education. (2013b, January). *California Common Core State Standards: Mathematics.* Sacramento, CA: Author. Accessed at https://cde.ca.gov/be/st/ss/documents/ccssmathstandardaug2013.pdf on February 19, 2022.

Collaborate. (n.d.). In *Merriam-Webster's online dictionary.* Accessed at https://merriam-webster.com/dictionary/collaborate on March 11, 2022.

Collins, J. (2001). *Good to great: Why some companies make the leap . . . and others don't.* New York: HarperBusiness.

Collins, J., & Porras, J. I. (1994). *Built to last: Successful habits of visionary companies.* New York: HarperBusiness.

Costa, A., & Kallick, B. (1993). Through the lens of a critical friend. *Educational Leadership, 51*(2), 49–51.

Covey, S. R. (1989). *The seven habits of highly effective people: Powerful lessons in personal change.* New York: Fireside.

Critical friend. (2013). In *The Glossary of Education Reform.* Accessed at https://edglossary .org/critical-friend on March 11, 2022.

Dimich, N. (2015). *Design in five: Essential phases to create engaging assessment practice.* Bloomington, IN: Solution Tree Press.

DuFour, R., DuFour, R., Eaker, R., Many, T. W., & Mattos, M. (2016). *Learning by doing: A handbook for Professional Learning Communities at Work* (3rd ed.). Bloomington, IN: Solution Tree Press.

DuFour, R., DuFour, R., Eaker, R., Mattos, M., & Muhammad, A. (2021). *Revisiting Professional Learning Communities at Work: Proven insights for sustained, substantive school improvement* (2nd ed.). Bloomington, IN: Solution Tree Press.

DuFour, R., & Eaker, R. (1998). *Professional Learning Communities at Work: Best practices for enhancing student achievement.* Bloomington, IN: Solution Tree Press.

DuFour, R., & Marzano, R. J. (2011). *Leaders of learning: How district, school, and classroom leaders improve student achievement.* Bloomington, IN: Solution Tree Press.

Eaker, R. (2020). *A summing up: Teaching and learning in effective schools and PLCs at Work.* Bloomington, IN: Solution Tree Press.

Eaker, R., & Keating, J. (2012). *Every school, every team, every classroom: District leadership for growing Professional Learning Communities at Work.* Bloomington, IN: Solution Tree Press.

Eaker, R., & Marzano, R. J. (Eds.). (2020). *Professional Learning Communities at Work and High Reliability Schools: Cultures of continuous learning.* Bloomington, IN: Solution Tree Press.

Erkens, C., Schimmer, T., & Dimich, N. (2017). *Essential assessment: Six tenets for bringing hope, efficacy, and achievement to the classroom.* Bloomington, IN: Solution Tree Press.

Fulton, K., & Britton, T. (2011, June). *STEM teachers in professional learning communities: From good teachers to great teaching.* Washington, DC: National Commission on Teaching and America's Future.

Hansen, A. (2015). *How to develop PLCs for singletons and small schools.* Bloomington, IN: Solution Tree Press.

Hattie, J. (2015). *What works best in education: The politics of collaborative expertise.* London: Pearson.

Kramer, S. V., & Schuhl, S. (2017). *School improvement for all: A how-to guide for doing the right work.* Bloomington, IN: Solution Tree Press.

Many, T. W., & Horrell, T. (2014). Prioritizing the standards using R.E.A.L. criteria. *TEPSA.* Accessed at https://smsdolc.files.wordpress.com/2018/06/priority -standards.pdf on February 19, 2022.

Marzano, R. J. (2003). *Classroom management that works: Research-based strategies for every teacher.* Alexandria, VA: Association for Supervision and Curriculum Development.

Marzano, R. J., Waters, T., & McNulty, B. A. (2005). *School leadership that works: From research to results.* Alexandria, VA: Association for Supervision and Curriculum Development.

Marzano, R. J. (2017). *The new art and science of teaching.* Bloomington, IN: Marzano Resources.

Mattos, M., DuFour, R., DuFour, R., Eaker, R., & Many, T. W. (2016). *Concise answers to frequently asked questions about Professional Learning Communities at Work.* Bloomington, IN: Solution Tree Press.

McTighe, J., & Wiggins, G. (2004). *Understanding by Design professional development workbook.* Alexandria, VA: Association for Supervision and Curriculum Development.

Moss, C. M., & Brookhart, S. M. (2019). *Advancing formative assessment in every classroom: A guide for instructional leaders* (2nd ed.). Alexandria, VA: Association for Supervision and Curriculum Development.

Muhammad, A. (2018). *Transforming school culture: How to overcome staff division* (2nd ed.). Bloomington, IN: Solution Tree Press.

Muhammad, A., & Cruz, L. F. (2019). *Time for change: Four essential skills for transformational school and district leaders.* Bloomington, IN: Solution Tree Press.

National Governors Association Center for Best Practices & Council of Chief State School Officers. (2010). *Common Core State Standards for English language arts and literacy in history/social studies, science, and technical subjects.* Washington, DC: Authors. Accessed at www.corestandards.org/assets/CCSSI_ELA%20Standards.pdf on March 15, 2022.

Schmoker, M. (2006). *Results now: How we can achieve unprecedented improvements in teaching and learning.* Alexandria, VA: Association for Supervision and Curriculum Development.

Senge, P. M. (1990). *The fifth discipline: The art and practice of the learning organization.* New York: Doubleday/Currency.

Spiller, J., & Power, K. (2019). *Leading with intention: Eight areas for reflection and planning in your PLC at Work.* Bloomington, IN: Solution Tree Press.

Waack, S. (2018). Collective teacher efficacy (CTE) according to John Hattie. *Visible Learning.* Accessed at https://visible-learning.org/2018/03/collective-teacher -efficacy-hattie on March 24, 2022.

Weger, H., Jr., Castle, G. R., & Emmett, M. C. (2010). Active listening in peer interviews: The influence of message paraphrasing on perceptions of listening skill. *International Journal of Listening, 24*(1), 34–49.

Wiliam, D. (2011). *Embedded formative assessment.* Bloomington, IN: Solution Tree Press.

Index

How to Develop PLCs for Singletons and Small Schools
Aaron Hansen
Ensure singleton teachers feel integrally involved in the PLC process. With this user-friendly guide, you'll discover how small schools, full of singleton teachers who are the only ones in their schools teaching their subject areas, can build successful PLCs.
BKF676

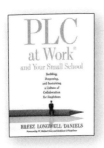

PLC at Work and Your Small School
Breez Longwell Daniels
Small schools can have a big impact. With the guidance of author Breez Longwell Daniels, an award-winning principal in Wyoming, your school will learn how to build a successful professional learning community (PLC) while staying true to its small-town roots.
BKF937

Learning by Doing
Richard DuFour, Rebecca DuFour, Robert Eaker, Thomas W. Many, and Mike Mattos
Discover how to transform your school or district into a high-performing PLC. The third edition of this comprehensive action guide offers new strategies for addressing critical PLC topics, including hiring and retaining new staff, creating team-developed common formative assessments, and more.
BKF746

Energize Your Teams
Thomas W. Many, Michael J. Maffoni, Susan K. Sparks, and Tesha Ferriby Thomas
Help your teams get better faster. Written for busy school leaders, instructional coaches, and teacher leaders, this ultimate "grab and grow" guide details how to bridge the gap between learning and doing at every stage of the PLC journey.
BKG009

Wait! Your professional development journey doesn't have to end with the last pages of this book.

We realize improving student learning doesn't happen overnight. And your school or district shouldn't be left to puzzle out all the details of this process alone.

No matter where you are on the journey, we're committed to helping you get to the next stage.

Take advantage of everything from **custom workshops** to **keynote presentations** and **interactive web and video conferencing**. We can even help you develop an action plan tailored to fit your specific needs.

Let's get the conversation started.

Call 888.763.9045 today.

SolutionTree.com